Learn to Play Keyboards

Learn to Play Keyboards
Steve Ashworth

CHARTWELL
BOOKS, INC.

A QUARTO BOOK

Published in 2008 by
Chartwell Books, Inc.
A division of Book Sales, Inc.
114 Northfield Avenue
Edison, New Jersey 08837
USA

Reprinted in 2009
Copyright © 2008 Quarto Inc.

ISBN-13: 978-0-7858-2365-0
ISBN-10 0-7858-2365-4
QUAR.LPK

This book was designed
and produced by:
Quarto Inc.
The Old Brewery
6 Blundell Street
London N7 9BH

Project Editor **Rachel Mills**
Assistant Editor
Chloe Todd Fordham
Managing Art Editor
Anna Plucinska
Photographer **Paul Forrester**
Illustrator **Kuo Kang Chen**
Sound Engineer **Phil Capone**
Art Director **Caroline Guest**

Creative Director **Moira Clinch**
Publisher **Paul Carslake**

Printed by Midas Printing Int'l Ltd.,
China
Color separation by Modern Age
Repro House Ltd., Hong Kong

Contents

Foreword

Learn to Play Keyboards is a self-tutorial for aspiring musicians. It will be invaluable to anyone learning keyboards for home-recording purposes or for songwriting inspiration, and especially those who want to play keyboards in a band. It focuses on a chord-based approach with rock and pop music as the main emphasis. This book demystifies the craft of music making, and gives you the confidence to play with other musicians on equal terms. I am confident that this book gives you all the information and inspiration you need to become the keyboard player you want to be.

Learning to play a musical instrument does not necessarily have to involve learning to read music. Many cultures around the world do not use musical notation, and there are many jazz, blues, rock, and folk musicians who cannot read a note of music. However, the advantages of being able to read a musical score are undeniable, so there are four sections in the book dedicated to explaining the mysteries of the written note.

Do you want to learn to play keyboards? If so, buy this book, study the lessons, practice the examples, join a band, and get out there and make some music!

About this book

The main section is made up of a series of short, simple lessons. Essential aspects of keyboard technique are covered as well as music notation, harmony, and the basic ingredients of different musical styles. Comprehensive chord and scale libraries will enable the reader to apply his knowledge to any song or playing situation.

The Lessons (pages 10–159)
The structured lessons will get you playing even if you have never touched a keyboard before, and include the first steps in reading music. Start at the beginning and work your way through. See over the page for how to use the various tools and notation in this book.

Chord Library (pages 160–209)
A comprehensive compendium of chords presented in easy-to-read diagrams and corresponding photographs, showing the three main chord types in all keys with relevant finger positions.

Scale Library (pages 210–225)
A library of all the scales introduced in the lessons, presented in diagram form to enable you to play the material in different keys.

A Brief History of Keyboards (pages 226–243)
An overview of the development of electric pianos, organs, and synthesizers; accompanied by a discography of classic recordings of these instruments.

Buyer's Guide (pages 244–249)
A guide to the myriad choice of contemporary electronic keyboards, with useful suggestions on finding an instrument to suit your requirements. Also a look at amplifiers, stands, cases, and other essential accessories.

Fold-out flap
Opposite page 255, you'll find a useful fold-out flap with an at-a-glance key to understanding musical notation. Keep it open at all times until you become more familiar with reading music.

The CD
You will find the accompanying CD an invaluable tool in working through this book, as it contains many of the key musical exercises actually being played, All of the exercises that can be heard on the CD are denoted with the relevant track number.

The Lessons (pages 10–159)

Chord Library (pages 160–209)

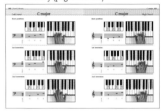

Scale Library (pages 210–225)

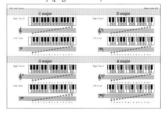

A Brief History of Keyboards (pages 226–243)

Buyers Guide (pages 244–249)

Using the graphics

The Lessons

Beginners should start at lesson 1 and work their way through.

If notes are to be played together, the keys to be played are shown grouped in one graphic. Blue tint indicates treble clef, and right hand.

Musical notes are identified on the graphic keyboard and beneath the notes being played.

Musical notation
Above and below each musical stave are keyboard diagrams that correspond to the notes being played by the right and left hand. Throughout the book: blue denotes right hand, and green left hand.

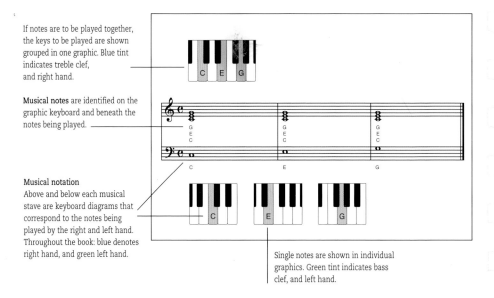

Single notes are shown in individual graphics. Green tint indicates bass clef, and left hand.

Left and right hand
This key indicates the range of the left and right hand on the musical notation. It corresponds with the green and blue graphics on the locator.

Keyboard locator
This device shows where on the keyboard the note or notes are being played, and whether the music relates to the left or right hand only, or both.

Left hand | Right hand

Right hand: C–G
Left hand: C–G

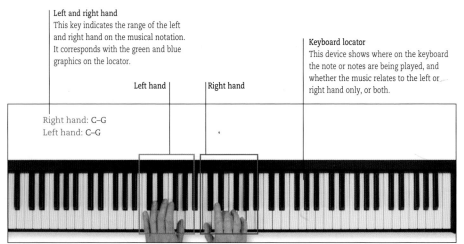

The Chord Library

The chords are organized by skill level, with the easiest ones first.

The keys to play are colored to indicate bass and treble clef, and left or right hand.

Numbers indicate which fingers to use (see page 13).

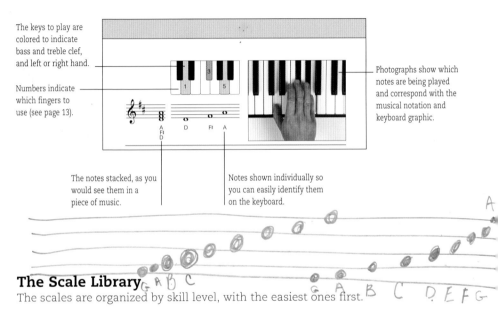

Photographs show which notes are being played and correspond with the musical notation and keyboard graphic.

The notes stacked, as you would see them in a piece of music.

Notes shown individually so you can easily identify them on the keyboard.

The Scale Library

The scales are organized by skill level, with the easiest ones first.

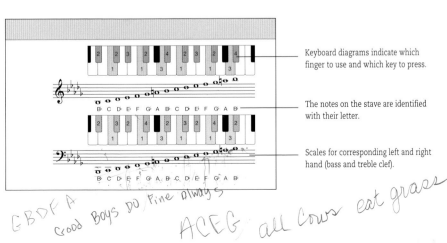

Keyboard diagrams indicate which finger to use and which key to press.

The notes on the stave are identified with their letter.

Scales for corresponding left and right hand (bass and treble clef).

The Lessons

The structured lessons will get you playing even if you have never touched a keyboard before, and include the first steps in reading music. Start at the beginning and work your way through. Later in the section, try out the musical genres, which include the blues, boogie-woogie, rock 'n' roll, and jazz.

1 Sitting at your keyboard

Being comfortable playing a keyboard is a matter of posture. The most important thing is to be as relaxed as possible, because any tension can cause muscular aches and pains.

Stevie Wonder, playing on "Top of the Pops" in the early 70s, demonstrates an ideal position for sitting at the keyboards.

Most keyboard players practice and perform from a sitting position, but some prefer to stand up, as this makes it easier to dance around on stage. When sitting down to play a keyboard, it is important to be at the right height in relation to the instrument. In general, a normal chair is too low for playing either a piano or a keyboard on a stand, which is why most keyboard players use a stool of some sort.

If you sit too low down, the temptation is to hunch your shoulders, which is not a relaxed posture and is likely to tire you quickly.

Sitting up straight is important because it is the most efficient way for your back to support the weight of your head. If you slouch forward, the weight of your head pulls your shoulders forward, which can lead to back ache and tiredness. These tips apply especially to practicing—when you're playing a gig you can do what you like!

Correct hand position

The correct hand position involves your fingers, wrists, arms, and all your body. The best technique will reduce extra movement and unnecessary strain, allowing you to play for hours at a time.

Fingers should be curved—a good reference is to put your hands on your knees when you are sitting at the keyboard, and to keep them in this shape while playing.

Finger numbers

In piano and keyboard notation the fingers are numbered 1 to 5, with the thumb being counted as finger number 1, and the little finger number 5. It is important to understand this system as most musical notation includes finger numbers to help you find the easiest way to play a new piece of music.

Rules to remember

- Sit centrally to the keyboard.
- Keep feet flat on the floor.
- Stay relaxed—keep those shoulders down!
- Keep your back straight.
- Sit at the correct height—thighs and forearms should be roughly horizontal.
- Keep your wrists flat.
- Curve your fingers.
- Touch the keys with the pads of your fingers—thumbs with the side of the pad.
- Long fingernails clatter on the keys and can upset the correct hand position—keep them short!

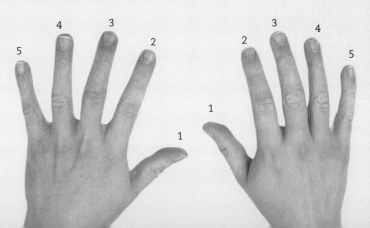

2 Keyboard layout

All pianofortes, fortepianos, harpsichords, synthesizers, xylophones, stylophones, organs, piano accordions, spinets, and celestas have the same keyboard layout. It consists of white and black keys with the black keys arranged alternately in groups of two and three.

The grouping of the black notes provides the key to identifying the notes. Where there is a group of two black keys the white note to the left is C. Once you have found C the other white notes are easy to find as they are arranged alphabetically from A to G and then back to A again. This pattern repeats up and down the keyboard.

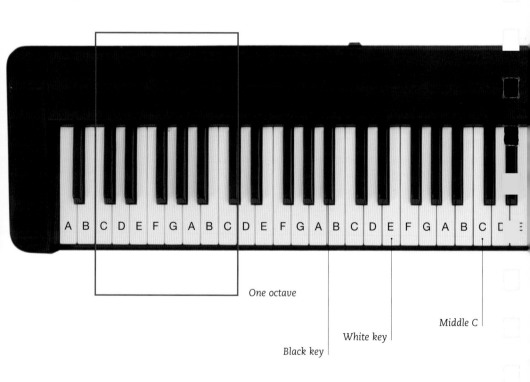

One octave

Middle C

White key

Black key

Low pitch

Try pressing keys at both ends of the keyboard. As you move to the right on a keyboard, the notes get higher in pitch, as you move to the left, they get lower. This means that your right hand is almost always playing higher-pitched notes than your left hand.

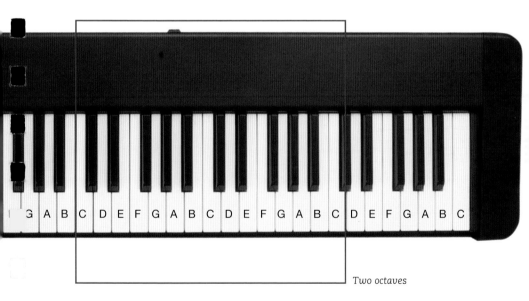

Two octaves

High pitch ⟶

3 Reading music 1: Notes

There are two things you need to know about a note: the pitch and the duration. This lesson deals with pitch. See Lesson 6, page 26, for more on duration.

SEE ALSO
Fold-out flap
Lesson 6, page 26

Music is written on a series of lines called a stave—most piano and keyboard music uses two staves joined together; one for the right hand and one for the left hand. The pitch of the note depends on its position on the stave. The higher the pitch of the note, the higher its position on the stave.

The treble clef is used for the upper part of keyboard music and is largely for right-hand notes.

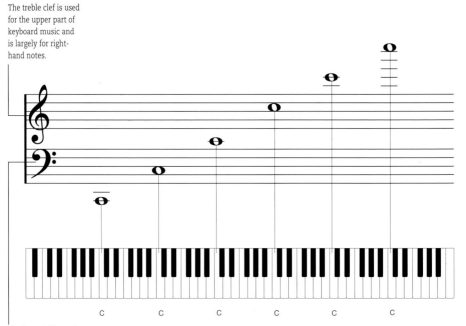

The bass clef is used for the lower part of keyboard music and is largely for left-hand notes.

Step 1

Don't expect to learn these straightaway but use this diagram as a reference when you need it. On the next page there are a couple of tricks to help you remember the notes in both clefs.

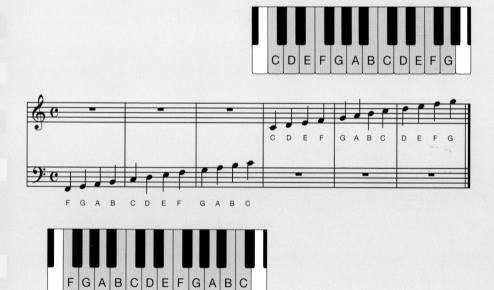

Right hand: **C–G**
Left hand: **F–C**

Lesson 3:
Reading music 1: Notes

Step 2

In the treble clef the notes that appear in the spaces spell FACE.

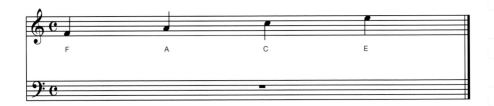

Step 3

In the bass clef, a phrase to help you remember the notes in the spaces is "All Cows Eat Grass."

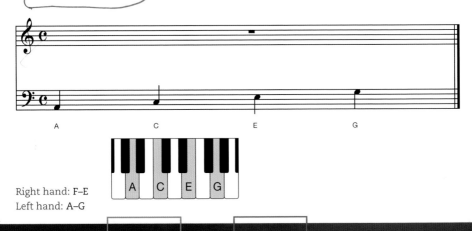

Right hand: F–E
Left hand: A–G

There are similar tricks to help you remember the notes on the lines.

Step 4

In the treble clef, a phrase to help you remember the notes on the lines is "Every Good Boy Deserves Football."

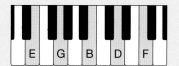

Every
Good
Boy
Does
Fine

Step 5

In the bass clef, a phrase to help you remember the notes on the lines is "George Bought Dolly Five Apples:"

Using these notes as a reference point you can count up and down alphabetically to work out other notes.

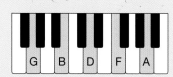

Good Boys
Do Fine
always

Right hand: E–F
Left hand: G–A

4 Right-hand chord shapes

On the CD
Track 1–3

SEE ALSO
Fold-out flap
Chord Library, *page* 160

Chords are groups of notes played together to create harmony. When different chords are played in succession you get a chord sequence, or chord progression, which can easily become a song or track.

Step 1 track 1

The most common chords are three-note chords called triads.

Here is a C major triad:

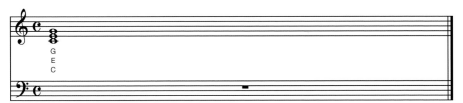

Play the C with your thumb and hold it down. Then play E with your third finger and hold down both notes. Then play G with your little finger and hold down all three notes. Then lift your hand off the keys and play all three notes together.

This shape of chord can be described as "play-a-note, miss-a-note, play-a-note, miss-a-note, play-a-note" and you can experiment with this chord shape starting on different notes (you don't always get a major chord though). A C major chord arranged in this way is said to be in "root position," as the first note is C, the "root" of the scale.

Right hand: **C–G**

Step 2 *track 2*

Because this chord has three notes you can play it in three different ways.
Here it is with E at the bottom:

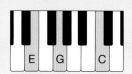

This time play E with your thumb and hold it down. Then play G with your second finger and hold it down. Then play C with your little finger and hold down all three notes. Then lift your hand off the keys and play all three notes together. The chord contains the same notes but in a different order, and is called an "inversion." The first note is E which is the third note of the scale—this progression is known as the "first inversion."

Step 3 *track 3*

There is one more variation:

Repeat the same process as step 2, but hold down G with your thumb. G is the fifth note of the scale—this progression is known as the "second inversion."

When you play the chords, listen to the sound of the notes and also look carefully at your hand to see the pattern your fingers make. Music is all about patterns.

5 Left-hand notes

On the CD
Track 4–7

SEE ALSO
Fold-out flap
Chord Library, page 160

The role of the left hand is often to play a bass note to accompany a chord being played by the right hand.

Step 1 track 4
In the previous lesson we looked at a C major chord so the most obvious note for the left hand to play is a C:

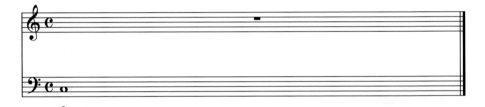

C

Left hand: **C**

Step 2 *track 5*

Now try both hands together:

Try to play all four notes (three right-hand and one left-hand) exactly together.

A note about being left-handed:

Left-handed guitarists have the luxury of being able to play left-handed guitars or right-handed ones turned upside-down. Left-handed keyboard players do not have this option—their right hands just have to work a bit harder. The same applies for right-handed players' left hands.

Right hand: C–G
Left hand: C

Lesson 5:
Left-hand notes

Step 3 *track 6*

Another way to vary this is to use a different note from the
C major chord as your bass note. Apart from C, there are two
other possibilities: the E and the G (the third and fifth notes
of the scale):

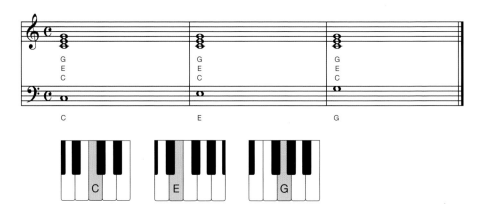

You will probably find that you prefer the sound of certain combinations to others.

Right hand: C–G
Left hand: C–G

Step 4 *track 7*

A reliable method to beef up the left-hand notes is to play an extra note, an octave lower or higher, together with the one you're already playing. Depending on the size of your hand, an octave can be a bit of a stretch, but it becomes more manageable with practice. The next example is the same as the previous one but with an F chord instead, and the left hand playing octaves.

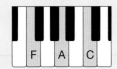

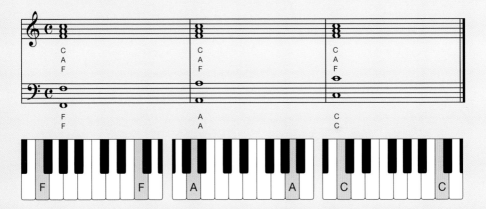

Right hand: F–C
Left hand: F–C

6 Reading music 2: Rhythm

On the CD
Track 8–16
SEE ALSO
Fold-out flap
Lesson 3, page 16

In lesson 3 we looked at how musical notation deals with the pitch of a note, and here we are going to see how the length, or duration, of notes is depicted.

Time signatures

Written music is divided into measures, and each measure represents a certain amount of time, depending on the time signature.

This time signature represents four beats (the top number), and each beat is a quarter beat (the bottom number.)

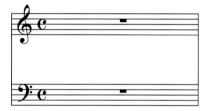

The "C" in this time signature stands for "common," and represents the 4/4 time signature, which is used most frequently.

The notes

A note is a symbol that represents a sound of a specific length. Take some time to memorize the table below, which shows the most commonly used notes, their different names, and their values (in beats).

Note	American Name	European Name	Value
o	Whole-note	Semibreve	4 beats
♩	Half-note	Minim	2 beats
♩	Quarter-note	Crotchet	1 beat
♪	Eighth-note	Quaver	½ beat
♪	Sixteenth-note	Semiquaver	¼ beat
♪	Thirty-second-note	Demi-semiquaver	⅛ beat

Here are some examples of rhythms using a mixture of half-notes, eighth-notes, and quarter-notes.

The first example shows four measures of quarter notes, which should be played completely evenly. Have a go at playing them first and then listen to the CD to see how close you were.

Step 1 track 8

Step 2 track 9

Step 3 track 10

These examples are written on the A above middle C. However, you could play any note, or clap, or tap—it's the rhythm that matters.

The rests

A rest is a symbol that represents a silence of a specific length; a gap between notes. Take some time to memorize the table below, which shows the most commonly used rests, their names, and their values (in beats).

Note	American Name	European Name	Value
▬	Whole-note rest	Semibreve rest	4 beats
▬	Half-note rest	Minim rest	2 beats
𝄽	Quarter-note rest	Crotchet rest	1 beat
𝄾	Eighth-note rest	Quaver rest	½ beat
𝄿	Sixteenth-note rest	Semiquaver rest	¼ beat
𝅀	Thirty-second-note rest	Demi-semiquaver rest	⅛ beat

Lesson 6:
Reading music 2: Rhythm

Dotted notes

So far you have become familiar with the twelve different notes and rests most commonly used in musical notation.

There are occasions when it is necessary to represent sounds (or indeed silences) of different lengths than those represented by these. One of the ways that this is achieved is through the use of dotted notes.

When a note or rest is attended by a dot, the value of that note is increased by 50 per cent. So for example, a whole-note has a value of four beats. If it is "dotted" and its value increases by 50 per cent, then its new value must be six beats. The table below shows the values of the dotted notes:

𝗼.	6 beats	▬:	6 beats
𝅗𝅥.	3 beats	▬.	3 beats
♩.	1½ beats	𝄽·	1½ beats
♪.	¾ beat	𝄾·	¾ beat

Although it is possible to add dots to both sixteenth-notes and thirty-second notes, neither is common, so they have not been included here. As well as the materials introduced previously, the following exercises include dotted quarter-notes.

Step 1 *track 11*

Step 2 *track 12*

Step 3 *track 13*

Tied notes

On the opposite page you discovered how dots are used to change the value of a note or rest. Another way in which sounds of different durations can be represented is through the use of tied notes.

When two or more notes are tied together, they are treated as a single note whose value is equal to the sum of the individual notes. So for example, if a whole-note (with a value of four beats) is tied to a half-note (with a value of two beats) they would be treated as a single note with a value of six beats (four beats plus two beats).

The table below shows some common combinations of tied notes.

Metronome

A metronome is an extremely useful tool for practicing rhythms, and some keyboards have one built-in. The numbers on a metronome stand for beats per minute (BPM), so a setting of 60 BPM is one beat per second, 120 BPM is two beats per second, and so on. Most music has a tempo marking at the top, which will be in BPM.

6 beats	3 beats	2 beats	1$^{1}/_{2}$ beat	1 beat

The following exercises involve the use of tied quarter-notes and eighth-notes.

Step 1 *track 14*

Step 2 *track 15*

Step 3 *track 16*

7 Basic "comping" patterns

On the CD
Track 17–19
SEE ALSO
Fold-out flap
Lesson 4, page 20
Lesson 5, page 22

In the previous lessons we have looked at how to form a chord and play a bass note to go with it. The next step is to use the chord to play a rhythmic pattern, which is referred to here as a "comping" pattern. This is very similar to the way in which a guitarist will strum a chord to create an accompaniment for a singer, or to jam with other musicians.

You need to have practiced the chords in lesson 4 and the left-hand notes in lesson 5 because now it's time to combine them.

Step 1 track 17

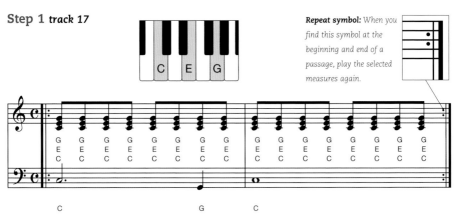

Repeat symbol: *When you find this symbol at the beginning and end of a passage, play the selected measures again.*

Right hand: C–G
Left hand: G–C

To make this sound good, play the repeated chords very evenly to create a strong rhythmic pulse. Take your time to work out where the left-hand notes fit in, and practice as slowly as you need to. It is important that right-hand and left-hand notes which come together are played exactly together.

The next step uses the same notes but introduces a different chord pattern.

Step 2 *track 18*

The right-hand pattern needs to be practiced very slowly and deliberately. Make sure that your third and fifth fingers play exactly together and that your thumb plays the note on its own. When you get the hang of it, add the left hand notes, which are exactly the same as in Step 1.

Practice tip

- When tackling a piece of music, always play **hands separately** to start with. Once you know which hands are playing which notes, play them together.

- If your hands are not obeying your brain, **slow down**. It's not a performance, and no-one's listening, so take your time.

Right hand: C–G
Left hand: G–C

Lesson 7:
Basic "comping" patterns

Now let's try the same thing with a different chord.

Step 3 *track 19*
Your fingers are doing exactly the same thing as in Step 2 but on different notes.

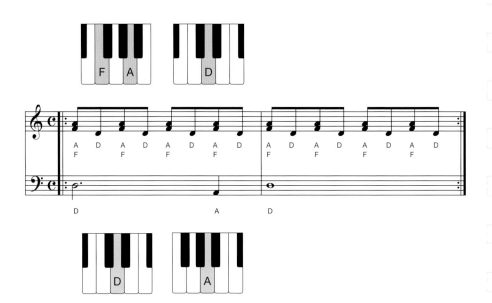

Right hand: D–A
Left hand: A–D

If you combine the chords from Step 2 and Step 3 then the result sounds much more musical.

Step 4

This short piece of music contains several essential aspects of keyboard playing, so spend time on it to get it perfect. The steadier the rhythm the better it will sound.

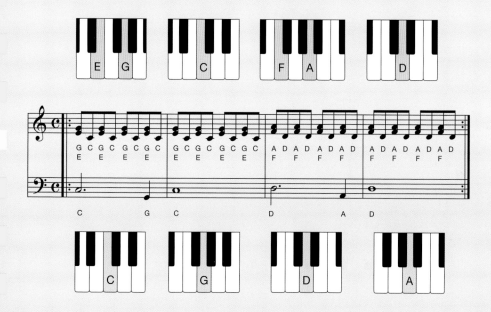

Right hand: C–A
Left hand: G–D

8 Three-chord trick

There are many songs that can be played using just three chords, and a chord progression of this type is often called a "three-chord trick."

On the CD
Track 20–21

SEE ALSO
Fold-out flap
Chord Library, *page 160*

In the key of C major, the three chords used would be C, F, and G. These are called the primary chords and are the most commonly used chords in that key.

Playlist

Here are some famous three-chord tracks:

"Heartbreak Hotel" **Elvis Presley**
"Johnny B. Goode" **Chuck Berry**
"Bye Bye Love" **The Everly Brothers**
"Twist and Shout" **The Beatles**
"Wild Thing" **The Troggs**
"Rock and Roll" **Led Zeppelin**
"Blowin' in the Wind" **Bob Dylan**
"I Wanna be Sedated" **The Ramones**
"I'm Gonna Be (500 Miles)" **The Proclaimers**
"Hotel Yorba" **The White Stripes**

Step 1 *track 20*

Here is an example using just the right hand:

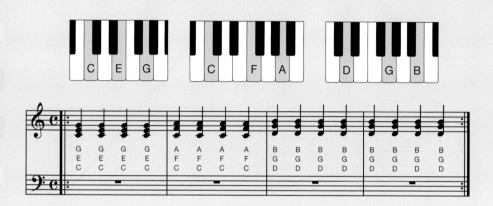

The chord in the first bar is C major as in lesson 4. The chord in the second bar is F major second inversion (see page 21). Notice that when you change to this chord your thumb stays on C and the other two notes move up a step.

Then, when you change to the chord in the third bar, which is G major second inversion, all the notes move up a step. Practice these moves very slowly and deliberately until you feel confident about which notes you are playing. When you've practiced the movement of the notes, play them in time, keeping a strong, regular beat. Listen to the CD if you're not sure of the rhythm.

Right hand: C–B

Lesson 8:
Three-chord trick

Step 2 *track 21*

Here are the left-hand notes that go with the chords:

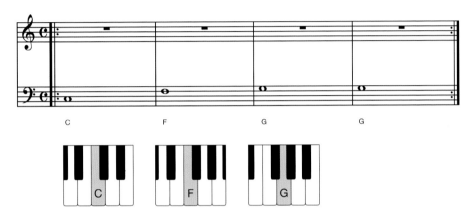

These are the "root" notes of the chords. So for the C chord the left hand plays a C, for the F chord the left hand plays an F, and so on. These are not the only left-hand notes that would fit with the chords, but they provide the most solid accompaniment.

Left hand: C–G

Step 3

Now try with both hands together:

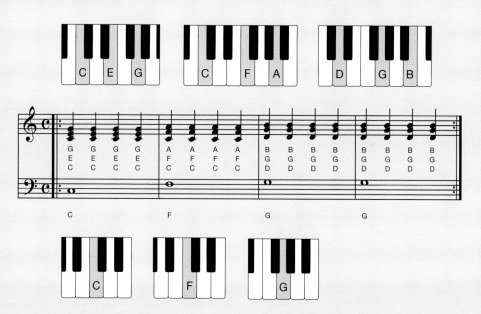

There are several different ways to practice this example. You have already played both hands separately. Another way is to play the whole thing with both hands from beginning to end. Alternately, you can play one bar at a time as a kind of loop, over and over. Another way is to isolate the most difficult parts and concentrate on them—in this example that would mean changing from one chord to the next. It is very useful to break up your practice in this way so that if you ever get into difficulty, you can switch to a different task. Also, listening to the CD will help you focus on what you're aiming for.

Right hand: C–B
Left hand: C–G

9 *Major and minor*

On the CD
Track 22–23

SEE ALSO
Fold-out flap
Scale Library, *page 210*
Lesson 8, *page 34*

The harmonic content of all Western music can be roughly organized into major harmonies and minor harmonies. These elemental forces indictate the tonality of a piece of music and determine its mood.

Broadly speaking, major is brighter, happier, and more outgoing than minor, which is darker and more brooding. These are very general characteristics and, as with most things in music, there are many gray areas and contradictions to confuse you along the way. Remember, music is an art form and as such resists classification.

Major and minor distinctions apply mainly to chords and scales. Three major chords were covered in Lesson 8 (see page 34), so in this lesson we move onto a couple of minor chords.

Major and minor songs

Famous songs in a major key:

"Fast Car" **Tracy Chapman**
"In the Light" **Led Zeppelin**
"Tears in Heaven" **Eric Clapton**
"Every Breath You Take" **The Police**
"Faith" **George Michael**
"Yellow" **Coldplay**
"Like a Rolling Stone" **Bob Dylan**
"Should I Stay or Should I Go" **The Clash**
"Black or White" **Michael Jackson**
"Let's Get it On" **Marvin Gaye**
"Cactus Tree" **Joni Mitchell**
"(Sittin' on) the Dock of the Bay"
Otis Redding

Famous songs in a minor key:

"Hotel California" **The Eagles**
"Sultans of Swing" **Dire Straits**
"Like a Prayer" **Madonna**
"Another Brick in the Wall" **Pink Floyd**
"Come Together" **The Beatles**
"Symphony No. 9" **Beethoven**
"Oye Como Va" **Santana**
"Losing My Religion" **R.E.M.**
"I Shot the Sheriff" **Bob Marley**

Step 1 *track 22*

Here, there are three-note chords in the right hand with a root note in the left hand. Take your time to find the correct notes and check the CD if you're not sure. As you play the chords, listen carefully to them and see if you agree that they sound meaner and moodier than the major chords in Lesson 8.

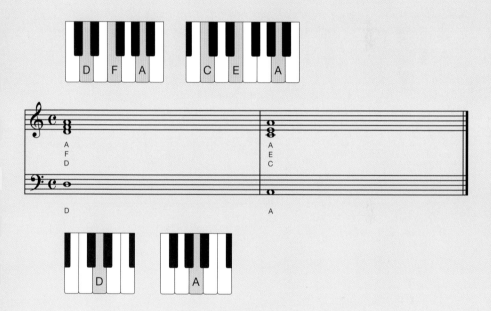

Right hand: C–A
Left hand: A–D

Lesson 9:
Major and minor

Step 2 *track 23*

If you're confident playing these chords then try the next example, which uses them to create a "comping" pattern similar to lesson 7:

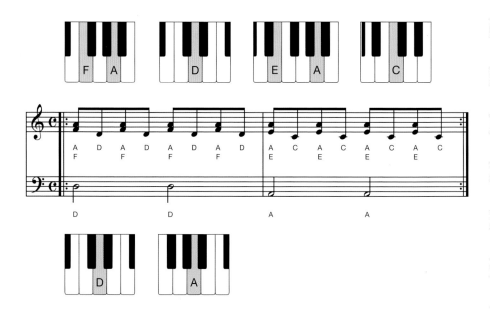

Right hand: C–A
Left hand: A–D

Step 3

Now you can use the chords that you have learned so far to create a chord sequence that combines major and minor chords, and is much more musically interesting.

This example is a piece of music with four measures, and one chord per measure. The order of the chords can be changed to create a different chord sequence, so experiment to see whether you can improve on the example given.

As you practice, always be aware of the importance of concentrating on the task at hand. If you feel yourself "drifting" try varying what you're doing—choose a different keyboard sound or change the lighting.

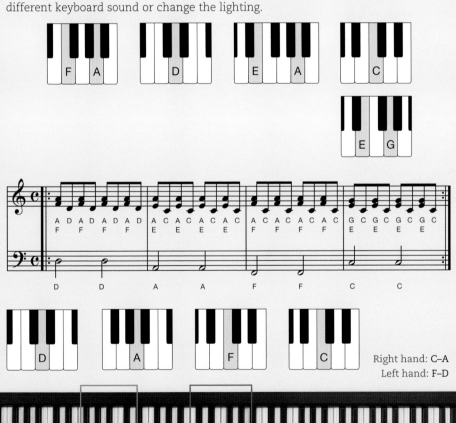

Right hand: C–A
Left hand: F–D

10 Reading music 3: Sharps and flats

SEE ALSO
Fold-out flap

It's time to delve further into the world of music notation, and here we look at sharps and flats.

Sharps and flats

The system so far covers all the white notes on the keyboard. The black notes are indicated either by a sharp sign (♯) or a flat sign (♭). On musical notation, these signs appear at the start of the music, or before the note they refer to (known as an accidental).

♯ A sharp sign indicates that the note has to be raised by a semitone. In most cases, this is the black note to the right. To help remember this, think of: Sharpen up.

♭ A flat sign indicates that the note must go down by a semitone. In most cases, this is the black note to the left. To help remember this, think of: Flatten down.

♮ A natural sign indicates the note must be played normally. Ignore the key signature at the start of the music, or a previous accidental in the measure.

Key signatures

Very often a piece of music will use the same sharps or flats all the way through, or at least for large sections, in which case we use a key signature. The key signature is written at the start of the music and shows the sharps or flats that will be used throughout the piece. These sharps or flats then no longer need to be written for individual notes.

A sharp or flat written on the key signature applies to that note wherever it is written on the stave. For instance, the key signature here has a B♭, which must be applied to all B notes throughout the piece.

B♭ is applied to every octave on the stave.

Organizing sharps and flats

Sharps and flats always appear in the same order on the key signature. The order of flats is the reverse order of sharps.

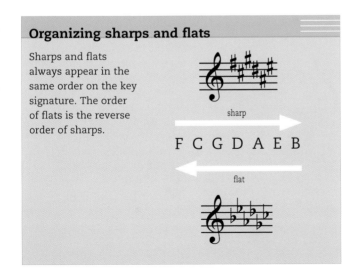

sharp

F C G D A E B

flat

Lesson 10:
Reading Music 3: Sharps and flats

Cycle of fifths

The key signature tells you what key the piece is in, as each key has its own unique key signature. As you start to learn the key signatures for each key a pattern begins to emerge that makes it easier to learn the key signatures.

You can organize the keys in terms of how many sharps or flats they have. The diagram on the opposite page is known as the cycle, or circle, of fifths. Starting with the key of C at the top of the circle, a sharp is added to each key signature as you follow it clockwise. The curious thing is that each key starts on the fifth step of the previous key, hence the name, cycle of fifths.

As you follow it anti-clockwise, a flat is added to each key signature. This time each key begins on the fourth step of the previous key.

The circle also works for minor keys. The letters inside the circle represent the relative minors, for example, C major and A minor share the same key signature—they have no sharps or flats.

As you can see, F♯ and G♭ share the same position at the bottom of the diagram. F♯ has six sharps and G♭ has six flats, and despite having different key names, note names, and key signatures, they are in fact the same notes. For this reason, I have only included G♭ major in the Chord Library and Scale Library, as the scales and chords would sound exactly the same. In musical terms we would say that they are enharmonics of each other. Play G♭ on your keyboard, then play F♯ to see this idea in action.

There is a strange logic and symmetry to this pattern, which is easy to grasp and use on a practical level, but difficult to understand why it actually works. It is an invaluable tool for understanding how the different keys relate to each other, and will help your understanding of key signatures.

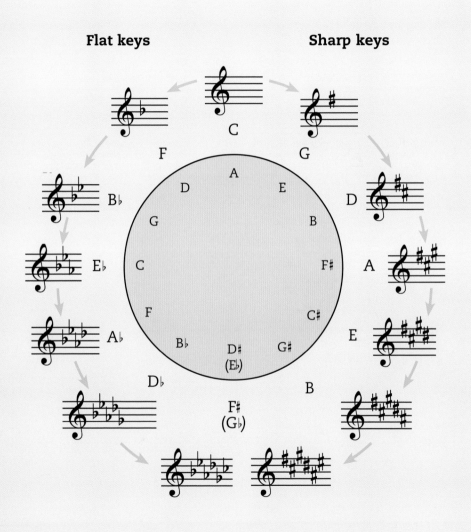

11 Major and minor scales

On the CD
Track 24
SEE ALSO
Fold-out flap
Scale Library, page 210

*Very few pieces of music use all the black and white
notes that are available, but a selection of them.
When these notes are arranged in order of pitch they
form a scale.*

Major scales

When a piece of music is based on the notes from a
particular scale it is said to be in that key, so a tune using
the notes from a C major scale is in the key of C major.

Step 1 *track 24*
The most common scale is a C major scale, which uses just
the white notes on the keyboard from C, to C an octave
higher. Practice this scale, playing one note after the other in
a continuous, smooth sequence.

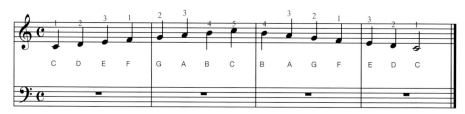

Right hand: C–C

The challenge of playing scales on the keyboard is not to run out of fingers, as there are more notes in the scale than fingers on your hand.

The finger pattern is crucial to success here and it involves an important technique known as "thumb under." As you play the example in step 1, the first three notes are played with your thumb, second finger, and third finger. Keep your third finger on E and move your thumb under onto the next note—F. This maneuver is worth practicing very slowly and carefully. Once your thumb is on F, carry on up the scale until you reach the next C with your little finger. On the way down, when you reach F with your thumb, the third finger crosses over onto E, and then you continue to C with your thumb.

It's a complicated explanation but this technique is fundamental to keyboard playing. As you play through a couple of times you will find it becomes easier. See below and turn to page 212 for photographs demonstrating this technique.

Step 2
Now try the left hand, playing one note after the other in a continuous, smooth sequence.

Here you start with the little finger of your left hand and the pattern is a mirror image of your right-hand pattern.

Left hand: C–C

Lesson 11:
Major and minor scales

Step 3

All scales except C major use at least one black note
(a sharp or flat), so let's have a look at one of those:

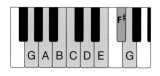

This is a G major scale and it has an F♯ in it. The finger pattern is the same as for the C major scale so you play G, A, and B with fingers 1, 2, and 3, then bring your thumb under on C. Then you have D and E with 2 and 3, and then F♯ with 4. The important thing here is to miss out the F and reach up to the F♯.

Practice this scale, playing one note after the other in a continuous, smooth sequence.

Right hand: **G–G**

Step 4
Now the left hand:

Again, this process is the mirror image of the right hand.
Practice this scale playing one note after the other in a
continuous, smooth sequence.

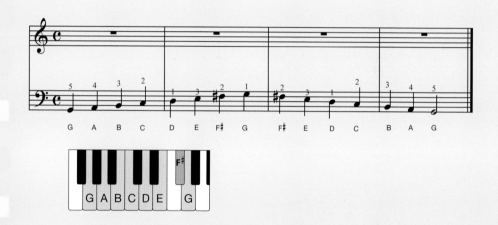

Left hand: G–G

Lesson 11:
Major and minor scales

Minor scales

Every major key has a minor counterpart that shares the same key signature, and is called the relative minor. For example, both F Major and D Minor have one flat (B♭), so D Minor is said to be the relative minor of F Major. The Cycle of fifths diagram on page 45 shows all the relative minors.

Step 5

The relative minor of C major is A minor, and if you play a scale starting from A, containing the notes of a C major scale, you get A♮ minor.

Natural minor scale: A

Right hand: A–A

Step 6

There are two other widely used minor scales; the melodic minor and the harmonic minor. The melodic minor has different notes ascending and descending.

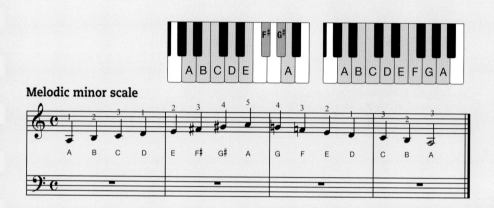

Melodic minor scale

The descending part of this scale is the same as the natural minor but the ascending part has a major 6th and major 7th step.

The harmonic minor scale is the same as the natural minor but with the seventh step raised by a semitone (see page 42). The notes of the harmonic minor are the same ascending and descending. This raised note is not shown in the key signature, which is why most harmonic minor scales have an "accidental" in them—sharpened or flattened notes that are not denoted by the key signature.

The minor scales in the Scale Library (see pages 220–225) are all harmonic minor scales, and if you look through them you will see that the seventh step of the scale always has a sharp sign or natural sign next to it.

Right hand: A–A

12 More "comping"

On the CD
Track 25–29

SEE ALSO
Fold-out flap
Lesson 7, page 30
Chord Library, page 160

*There are many different ways to play a chord
accompaniment on the keyboard, even if you're
using the same chord progression. By using different
rhythmic patterns, and combinations of notes, you
can create different styles and moods, from mellow
ballads to fast rock.*

Step 1 track 25
This example uses an arpeggio pattern. This is a type of broken chord, which is
exactly what it says, a chord broken into single notes. This type of pattern can
create a relaxing, dreamy mood:

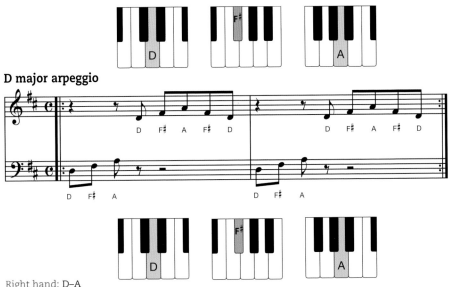

D major arpeggio

Right hand: D–A
Left hand: D–A

The notes in step 1 are all from a D major chord and both hands are playing it in root position. Have a look at the Chord Library, where the diagrams and photos will help you get your bearings (see page 160). Playing this smoothly and evenly will create the effect you want—keep repeating the pattern over and over until it feels really comfortable.

Step 2 track 26

This example is very similar but uses the notes from a B minor chord. The right hand is playing a first inversion chord shape, and the left hand is using an octave pattern:

B minor arpeggio

Right hand: D–B
Left hand: B–B

Lesson 12:
More "comping"

Step 3

When you combine the two examples from the previous two pages it creates a more interesting piece of music:

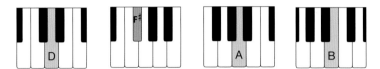

D major and B minor

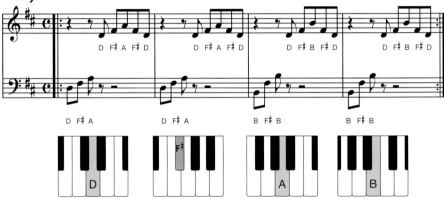

There is a change of hand position between measures 2 and 3, which you may find helpful to isolate and practice very slowly. The left-hand little finger has to stretch from a D down to a B and it would be a good idea to practice this just with your left hand.

One reason for using different chord inversions is to create smooth changes between the chords. In Step 3 the D major chord and B minor chord have two notes in common, which are D and F♯, so by using different inversions you can create a very smooth chord change. Most of the examples in the book can be varied by using different inversions—have a go!

Right hand: **D–B**
Left hand: **B–B**

Step 4 *track 27*

You can use exactly the same notes to create a pattern with a stronger beat:

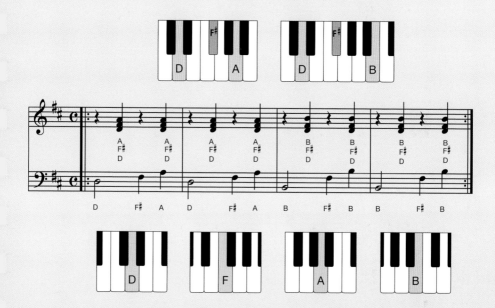

Go through this with hands separately to start with. When you put them together, notice that the last chord in each measure comes together with the left hand.

The left-hand note at the start of each measure has a natural accent because it is on the first beat of the measure, so give this note a bit more weight (play it louder). If you're unsure of the rhythms, check the track that goes with step 5.

Right hand: D–B
Left hand: B–B

Lesson 12:
More "comping"

Step 5 *track 27*

Extend this example by adding two more chords but keeping the same rhythmic pattern.

These two extra chords are G major and E minor. Again, have a look at the Chord Library to familiarize yourself with these chords. Practice the left hand on its own so that you can play through the whole sequence without hesitating, and then add the right hand chords.

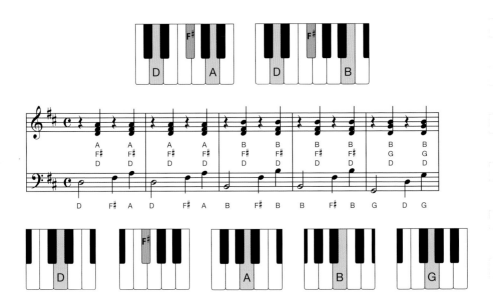

Right hand: **D–B**
Left hand: **G–B**

This number is the measure number, which is commonly used in musical scores to make navigating across different pages less tricky.

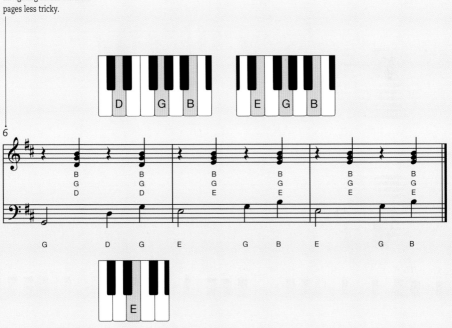

Lesson 12:
More "comping"

Step 6 *track 28*

This example uses a broken chord pattern in the right hand with bass notes in the left. The two chords here are G minor in measures 1 and 2, and F major in measures 3 and 4. Because these chords are in the key of F there is a B♭ in the key signature.

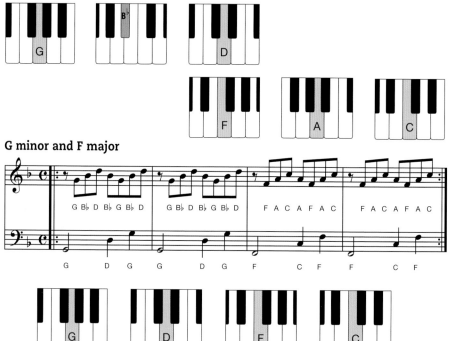

G minor and F major

Practice the left hand on its own carefully. A "stepping-stone" to playing the whole thing is to play all the left-hand notes and only the right-hand notes that come with the left hand. This is very useful as it helps you work out where your right and left hands are playing notes together.

Right hand: **F–D** Left hand: **F–G**

Step 7 *track 29*

The next example uses an E minor chord root position, and a B minor first inversion. The left-hand part has more rhythmic interest, and the right-hand chords come on the beats in between the left hand notes. Watch out for the F# in the key signature.

E minor and B minor

This rhythmic pattern features "off-beat" chords and is used extensively in reggae and ska music.

Style and genre

All rock and pop music derives from a variety of different sources. We are all used to hearing musicians naming their influences, whether a genre of music or a particular artist, and it is important to realize that nobody invents their own style from scratch. As a musician, it is essential to be open-minded and to have an awareness of different styles, even ones you're not primarily interested in. Having a working knowledge of jazz piano, for example, doesn't mean you have to play jazz—you can use elements of the style in different contexts to enrich your playing.

Right hand: D–B Left hand: B–E

13 Dominant seventh chords

Having looked at major and minor chords, the next most important chord type is the dominant seventh. This chord is a major triad (three-note chord) with a minor seventh. The seventh chord contains dissonance, which in musical terms means the chord sounds unstable and needs to resolve. This type of chord creates tension and movement;

Step 1 *track 30*

The seventh chord has a richer, more complex sound than a straightforward major chord, and is often used for this reason more than for its harmonic function.

In technical terms, the seventh chord is comprised of the root, major third, fifth, and flattened seventh of the scale, so the notes of a C7 chord are C, E, G, and B♭. The B♭ is the seventh and it is this note that gives the chord its personality.

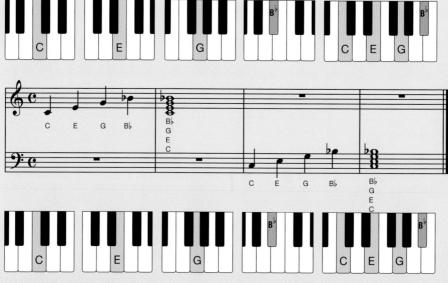

Right hand: C–B♭ Left hand: C–B♭

On the CD
Track 31–32

SEE ALSO
Fold-out flap
Chord Library, page 160

it asks questions and expects answers. A G7 chord would most commonly resolve to a C major chord—however in rock and pop music conventions are not so rigid, and seventh chords can often make up an entire chord sequence.

Step 2 *track 31*
Here's a rhythmic pattern using the chord. The right hand plays the chord in quarter-notes, while the left hand plays the root and seventh to create a bass line:

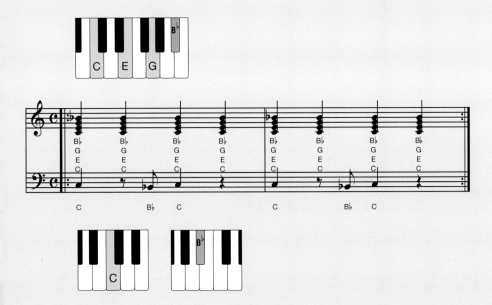

Right hand: C–B♭
Left hand: B♭–C

Lesson 13:
Dominant seventh chords

Step 3 *track 32*

This example is the same pattern as step 2, but with an F7 chord in the second inversion. Because the root and seventh are only a step away from each other the notes are very bunched up, and when they are written down the two that are next to each other are shown either side of the note stem. Don't let this put you off, the notes are all in the same chord and have to be played together:

This example shows notes on either side of the stem as otherwise they would overlap. Play together as normal.

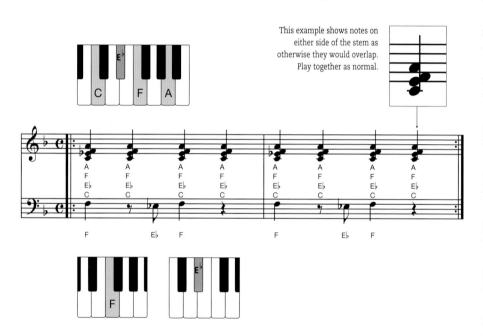

Right hand: C–A
Left hand: E♭–F

Step 4

Put these examples together to create a 4-bar pattern using two seventh chords:

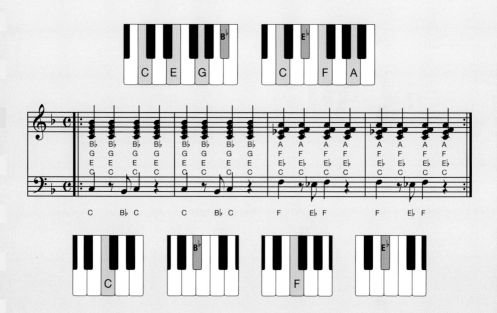

Changing between chords is more difficult now as there are four notes in each chord, so start with the right hand on its own, and change slowly from the C7 chord to the F7 chord. When you have mastered this, add the left-hand notes.

Right hand: C–B♭
Left hand: B♭–F

14 Pentatonic scales

On the CD
Track 33
SEE ALSO
Fold-out flap
Scale Library, page 210

Pentatonic scales contain five notes, rather than the seven in normal major and minor scales, and provide a great way to start improvising or soloing. There are innumerable pentatonic scales (choose any five notes and you've got one!), but the most common ones are shown here.

Step 1 track 33
The major pentatonic scale is made up of the first, second, third, fifth, and sixth degrees of the major scale, so a C major pentatonic scale looks like this:

Practice this scale, playing one note after the other in a continuous, smooth sequence.

Major pentatonic scale: C

Play any C major chord (see the Chord Library, page 160) with your left hand and the notes of the pentatonic scale with your right hand. All the notes fit easily with the chord so it's very difficult to play a "wrong" note. This makes pentatonic scales extremely good for improvising with.

Right hand: C–C

Step 2

The minor pentatonic scale is made up of the first, third, fourth, fifth, and seventh degrees of the scale, so an A minor pentatonic scale looks like this:

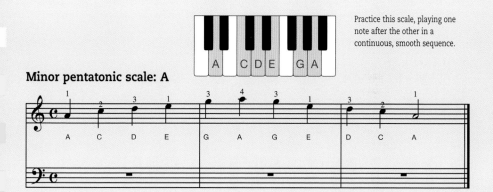

Practice this scale, playing one note after the other in a continuous, smooth sequence.

Minor pentatonic scale: A

Relative scales

Anyone paying close attention will notice that these two scales contain exactly the same notes but in a different order, which makes them versatile to use.

Right hand: A–A

15 Reading music 4: Changing key

On the CD Track 34

SEE ALSO
Fold-out flap
Lesson 10, *page 42*

*Changing from one key to another in music is called
transposing. There are many situations where music
needs to be transposed, and one of the most common
is where a singer needs a song to be higher or lower than the written
key. In this case the whole song has to be transposed including all
chords, bass lines, and keyboard parts.*

Step 1
The intervals between each note are what makes this a major scale NOT the
notes themselves. Check the major scales in the Scale Library (see page 160)
and you will find they all have the same pattern of intervals: tone (C–D),
tone (D–E), semitone (E–F), tone (F–G), tone (G–A), tone (A–B), semitone (B–C).

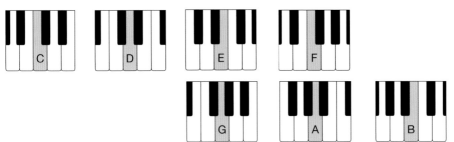

C major scale

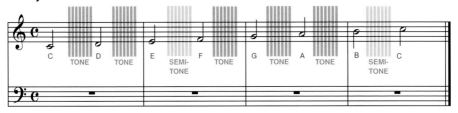

Right hand: C–C

Step 2 *track 34*

Here's a musical example in the key of C major:

Right hand: D–D Left hand: C–E

Lesson 15
Reading music 4: Changing key

Step 3

If you want to transpose the key of C major to D major, for example, you need to change the first note from C to D and then go up the scale, keeping the intervals between the notes exactly as they were in step 1.

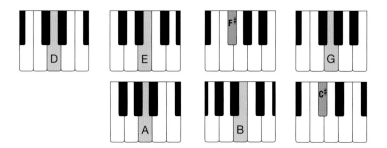

D major scale

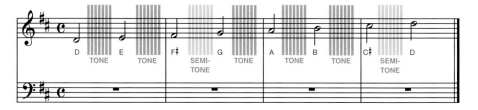

Notice that the F and the C have to be sharp, because otherwise the intervals would not be the same as in the C major scale in step 1.

Right hand: **D–D**

Step 4

This example is the transposed version of the musical example in C major. Notice that the key signature has C♯ and F♯, as step 3 explained. This key signature tells you that you are now in D major.

Simply move all the notes (the right-hand melody and the left-hand chords) up a whole tone—the difference between the C and D.

Right hand: E–E
Left hand: D–F♯

16 12-bar blues

The exact origins of the style of music known as the "blues" are obscure. It emerged from the work songs and spirituals of African-American slaves at the end of the 19th century and evolved into a recognizable form during the first half of the 20th century.

The 12-bar blues is a musical form that permeates Western music. It is a chord progression that provides the harmonic DNA for countless tracks in any contemporary genre you care to name: jazz, blues, gospel, country, rock 'n' roll, pop, and so on.

The blues is a common musical language that enables musicians to jam together without any rehearsal so it is essential that any aspiring musician is familiar with the 12-bar blues form.

In the following lessons we will look at the musical ingredients of the blues, including the fundamental chord progression, scales, and "licks" associated with the style.

Little Richard, USA, c.1955—a key figure in the transition between rhythm and blues and rock 'n' roll.

Playlist

The following tracks all use a 12-bar blues chord progression:

"Flying Home"
Lionel Hampton
"In the Mood"
Glenn Miller
"Honky-Tonk Train Blues"
Meade Lux Lewis
"Blue Monk"
Thelonious Monk
"Night Train"
Oscar Peterson

"Shake, Rattle and Roll"
Charles Calhoun
"Tutti Frutti"
Little Richard
"Rock Around the Clock"
Bill Haley
"See You Later Alligator"
Bobby Charles
"Hound Dog"
 Lieber and Stoller

"The Twist"
Hank Ballard
"Summertime Blues"
Eddie Cochran
"Green Onions"
Booker T and the MGs
"Rock and Roll"
Led Zeppelin
"Red House"
Jimi Hendrix

Lesson 16:
12-bar blues

On the CD
Track 35–36

SEE ALSO
Fold-out flap
Chord Library, *page 160*

*The basic chord progression for the blues is based
on the three primary chords, which are formed from
the first, fourth, and fifth steps of the scale. This
12-bar pattern is repeated over and over to create
a blues performance, with different instrumental
solos and vocal sections fitting over the repeated
chord pattern.*

Step 1 *track 35*

Starting with C major, the first chord is C, the fourth chord is F, and the fifth
chord is G, all in root position. These chords are played in a 12-bar sequence
shown below and continuing onto the page opposite.

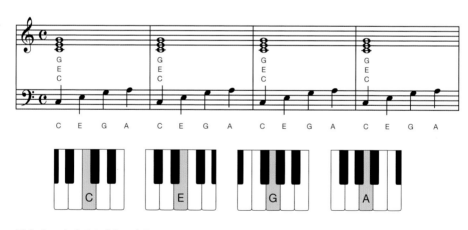

Right hand: C–D Left hand: F–A

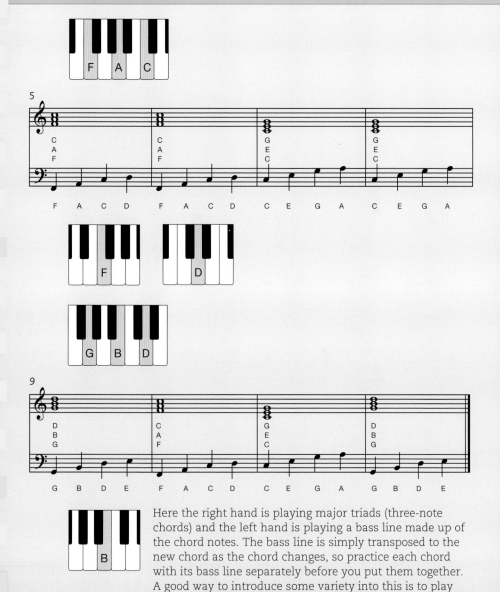

Here the right hand is playing major triads (three-note chords) and the left hand is playing a bass line made up of the chord notes. The bass line is simply transposed to the new chord as the chord changes, so practice each chord with its bass line separately before you put them together. A good way to introduce some variety into this is to play the right-hand chord more rhythmically, rather than just on the first beat of the bar.

Lesson 16:
12-bar blues

Step 2 *track 36*

Keyboard players and guitarists will often use dominant seventh chords
(see Lesson 13, page 60) rather than major chords in a blues progression, to
create more tension and movement. The next example contains left-hand
chords, with a right-hand melody on top.

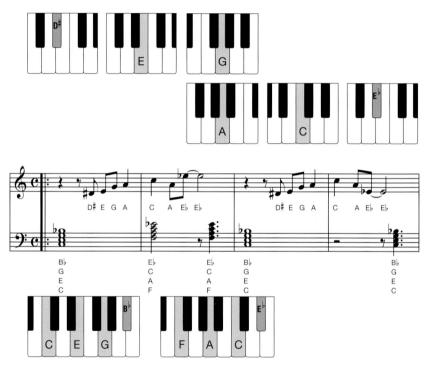

The left-hand chords are C7, F7, and G7. You will need to be confident of
the notes in these chords before adding the melody. The right hand has
lots of sharps and flats so take care to get the correct notes.

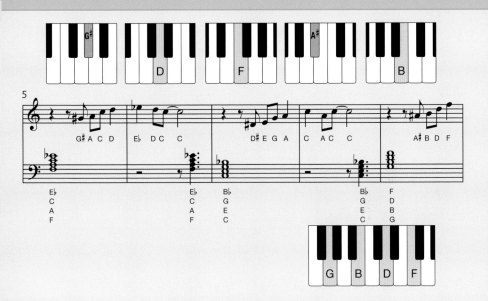

Right hand: D♯–F
Left hand: C–F

17 The blues scale

On the CD
Track 37–43

SEE ALSO
Fold-out flap
Lesson 14, page 64

The blues scale is a minor pentatonic scale with an added flattened fifth. The notes of the scale provide an easy "way in" to achieving a bluesy sound for improvising, but are not all there is to blues soloing. Endless "noodling" on a blues scale does not constitute fantastic blues playing, but is a useful way of finding your way around a blues progression.

Step 1 *track 37*

This is a C blues scale, which is a C minor scale with an added flattened fifth—the G♭.

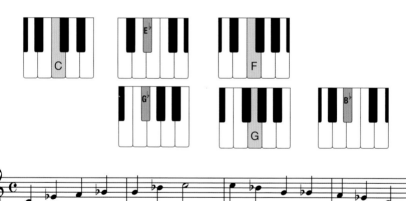

C   E♭   F   G♭ | G   B♭   C | C   B♭   G   G♭ | F   E♭   C

Right hand: C–C

Step 2 *track 38*

The first example here is a C7 and then an F7 chord in the left hand, and a C blues scale (as step 1) in the right hand.

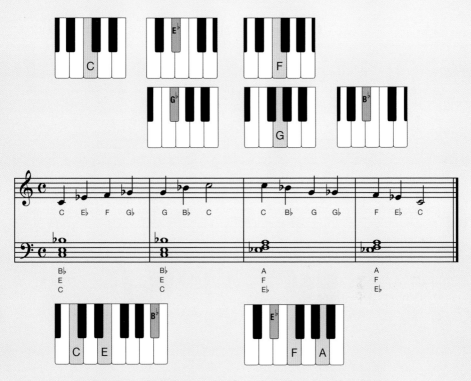

What is immediately striking is that the first chord has a major third (E), and the scale has a minor (E♭). This tension between major and minor thirds is a key element of the sound of the blues and one reason why the blues scale contains the notes that it does.

Right hand: C–C
Left hand: C–B♭

Lesson 17:
The blues scale

Step 3 *track 39*

The next example is a pattern based on the blues scale, first with a C7 chord and then with an F7 chord. This example shows how the blues scale can fit over different chords within a blues progression.

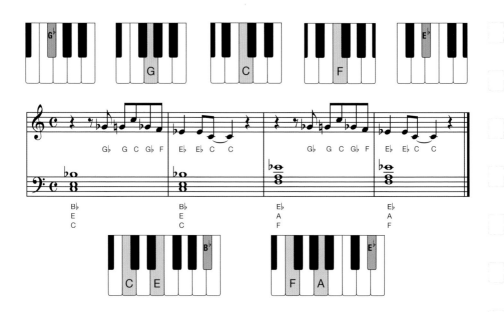

Right hand: C–C
Left hand: C–Eb

Step 4 *track 40*

A C blues scale can also fit over a C minor chord, as in this example:

Here there is no tension between the major and minor third but the flattened fifth (the G♭) gives the melody a bluesy sound.

So, the blues scale can be used over the chords in a blues sequence and also over a minor chord to create a bluesy sound. However it is a mistake to rely too heavily on the use of the blues scale; there are many other ways to approach the blues.

Right hand: C–E♭ Left hand: C–G

Lesson 17:
The blues scale

Blues licks

The blues progression provides a great way to work on your soloing skills, because you can expect anyone to know it, and just get on and play. The blues scale in the previous lesson is a fantastic tool for improvising, but you can build on that with the use of "licks." A lick is a short melodic line, or stock phrase, that can be used as part of a solo. It does seem strange that a solo, which is improvised, should contain bits that are already worked out, but in a way it is inevitable. A good analogy is with speech, where every sentence is spontaneous and quite possibly unique, but is peppered with commonly used phrases and expressions. In the same way, an improvised solo can be completely original but at the same time contain phrases that have been heard many times before. A skilled improviser will use a combination of licks, scale patterns, and spontaneous ideas to create an exciting and original solo.

Step 1 *track 41*

Many blues licks are based on the blues scale, and use techniques that are essential to the style, such as trills, runs, and crushed notes.

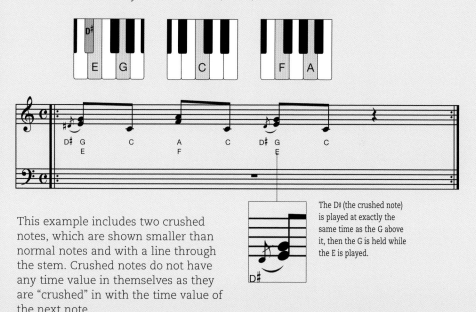

This example includes two crushed notes, which are shown smaller than normal notes and with a line through the stem. Crushed notes do not have any time value in themselves as they are "crushed" in with the time value of the next note.

The D♯ (the crushed note) is played at exactly the same time as the G above it, then the G is held while the E is played.

There are two ways to play this example. The first is to play the D♯ with your second finger and the G with your fifth. Then you hold the G and play the E right away with your third finger.

A slightly different method is again to play the D♯ with your second finger but this time play the G with your fourth finger. Now instead of playing the E with your third finger, slide your second finger down the side of the D♯ and onto the E. This technique is useful for playing crushed notes but can be difficult depending on the action of your keyboard. The thing to remember is that the crushed note is very quick and not really heard as a separate note in its own right.

Right hand: C–A

Lesson 17:
The blues scale

Step 2 *track 42*

The next example uses a D♯ and E, the major and minor thirds of the C chord on which this lick is based. This tension between major and minor thirds is a characteristic sound of the blues.

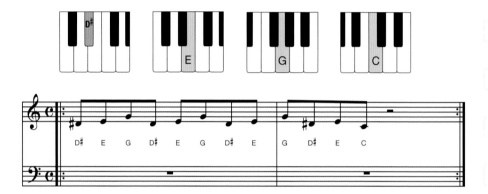

Try switching between "straight" and "swing" rhythm. "Straight" rhythm has the eighth-notes played evenly, exactly as written. "Swing" rhythm has a triplet feel, where two eighth-notes are played as the first and third notes of a triplet.

Right hand: C–G

Step 3 *track 43*
The next example uses the notes from the C blues scale.

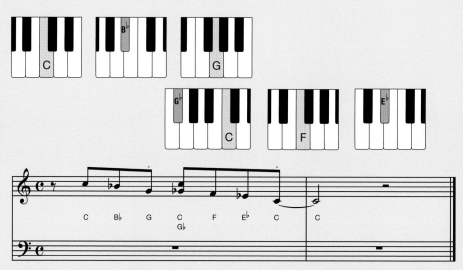

Start with your third finger on the C, then your second on B♭, and your thumb on G. Here your second finger crosses over onto the G♭ and you play this together with the C with your little finger. This interval is a flattened fifth and gives this lick a characteristic bluesy sound.

Practice these licks in different keys and see if you can extend the licks by adding more notes to create a longer phrase in the same style.

Right hand: C–C

18 Boogie-woogie

Boogie-woogie originated as a blues-based piano style, with a strong emphasis on driving rhythms for dancing, and was enormously popular throughout the 1930s and 1940s. As a style, it merged elements of honky-tonk, barrelhouse, and ragtime.

"Pinetop's Boogie-Woogie" and "Honky-Tonk Train Blues," recorded by Pinetop Smith and Meade Lux Lewis respectively in the late 1920s, were records that documented the arrival of the genre and anticipated much of what was to come. Swing bands and smaller groups adopted the boogie-woogie style, repeated bass figures and blues style improvisations, and are very "pianistic" in nature.

Boogie-woogie masters

The big three of boogie-woogie piano are Albert Ammons, Pete Johnson, and Meade Lux Lewis, who all enjoyed success throughout the 1930s and the war years. In the 1950s and 1960s the rhythm and drive of boogie-woogie influenced many blues performers and

had a massive impact on the birth of rock 'n' roll. Many jazz pianists incorporate elements of boogie-woogie into their playing—the Canadian jazz pianist virtuoso Oscar Peterson was a phenomenal exponent of the art. Boogie-woogie is still popular in its own right, with many performers continuing the tradition today.

Boogie-woogie bass lines

An essential ingredient of boogie-woogie is a repeated, driving bass line, and even if boogie-woogie isn't your favorite style, it will be useful to learn and practice some of the examples in this lesson. They are great for developing left-hand strength and independence, and very similar bass lines are used in blues and rock.

Playlist

This is a collection of phenomenal boogie-woogie tracks from 1928 onward.

"Pinetop's Boogie Woogie" **Pinetop Smith**
"Honky-Tonk Train Blues" **Meade Lux Lewis**
"Roll 'em Pete" **Big Joe Turner** and **Pete Johnson**

"Yancey Special" **Jimmy Yancey**
"Boogie-Woogie Stomp" **Albert Ammons**
"Dirty Dozens" **Speckled Red**
"Sticky Finger Boogie" **Ben Waters**

Meade Lux Lewis in 1954. Lewis helped establish boogie-woogie as a major blues piano style.

Lesson 18:
Boogie-woogie

On the CD
Track 44–49
SEE ALSO
Fold-out flap
Lesson 16, page 70

Step 1 *track 44*

These examples are intended to be played with a "swing" feel, but are written here as straight eighth-notes. Listen to the CD to get a feel for the rhythm if you're not sure.

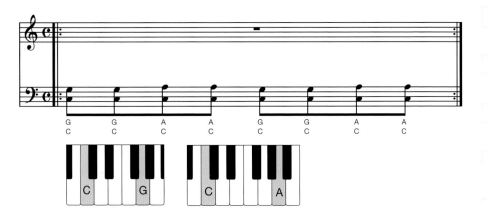

This is probably the most common of all boogie bass lines and is also a favorite with guitarists. The C is played with the little finger and the G with the second finger. Then, when the A and C are played together, the A is played with the thumb. The aim is to keep your wrist relaxed so that your hand can bounce off the keys without your fingers doing too much of the work. The bass line needs to be practiced around a 12-bar blues progression, which means this needs to be played in F and G as well (see steps 2 and 3).

Left hand: C–A

Step 2
This uses exactly the same fingering as in Step 1,
but the notes are different.

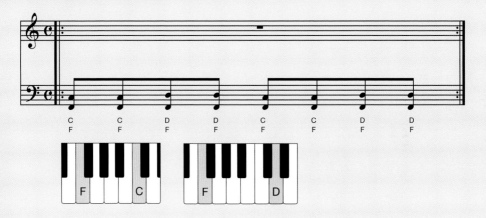

12-bar blues and boogie-woogie

It is worth noting that many early blues and boogie-woogie
performers didn't always play a 12-bar pattern—some included
8-bar, 4-bar, and even 10-bar sections—although this can create
problems if you're playing with other musicians!

Left hand: F–D

Lesson 18:
Boogie-woogie

Step 3

This also uses the same fingering as in Step 1, but again, the notes are different.

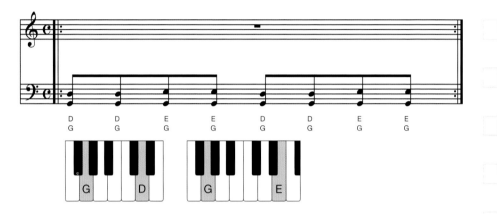

12-bar pattern

These three steps are the three patterns that you need to play a 12-bar pattern in C. Refer to the lesson on 12-bar blues progression to see how they fit together (see page 70).

Left hand: G–E

Here are some more typical boogie-woogie bass lines, but only in C, so you will need to transpose them to fit a 12-bar sequence (see page 72). Any of them can be changed, so do try some different variations—it is always worth alternating between a "straight" and "swing" rhythm to see which you prefer.

Step 1 track 45
This bass line is more melodic.

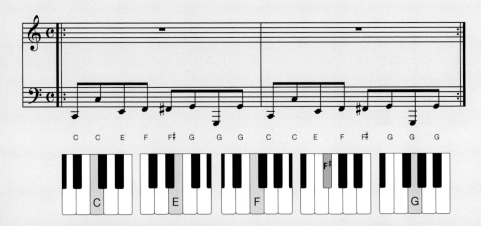

Bass lines

As with the first three steps, the examples on the following pages provide bass lines for a blues chord progression in C. The notes with accidentals (sharps and flats) are chromatic passing notes, which do not affect the key signature.

The octave leaps are very characteristic of boogie-woogie bass lines and can be quite tricky to negotiate. In this example the first note is with the little finger and then the octave C is played with the thumb. As you play the octave, roll (rotate) your wrist toward the note so that your thumb doesn't have to do all the work.

Left hand: G–C

Lesson 18:
Boogie-woogie

Step 2

This bass line is made up entirely of octave leaps so make sure your wrist is loose as you "roll" from little finger to thumb. This is extremely effective as an exercise for developing left-hand strength and agility, and is useful in many different genres.

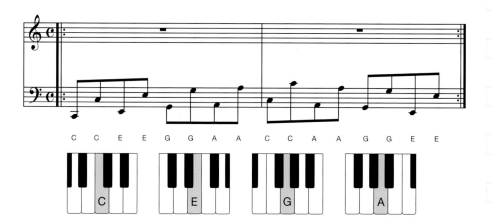

Left hand: C–C

Step 3

This pattern is a great workout for your left-hand little
finger—possibly the keyboard player's most neglected
digit. The repeated Cs at the start have to be struck very
cleanly, and with good control, to set up a strong beat at
the start of the bass line.

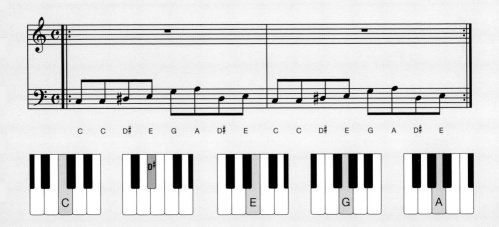

C C D♯ E G A D♯ E C C D♯ E G A D♯ E

Left hand: C–A

Lesson 18:
Boogie-woogie

Step 4 *track 46*

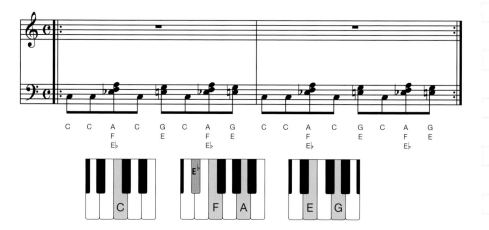

There are endless variations on these patterns and it is definitely worth practicing them to the point where you can achieve a steady beat. The challenge is to maintain a constant, driving pulse while keeping a relaxed arm and wrist to avoid "tightening-up." An even greater challenge is then to add a right-hand part!

Left hand: C–A

Boogie-woogie licks

The right hand plays blues-type licks that tend to be simpler and more repetitive than some other blues-related styles. This is partly due to the fact that you have to keep the left hand going at all costs!

Step 1 *track 47*

The first example is just two notes that are repeated in a triplet figure (three notes played in the time usually taken to play two—in this case the three eighth-notes are played in the time of two eighth-notes).

A triplet is a rhythmic grouping of three evenly spaced notes. Here, this triplet must be played in the time of two beats.

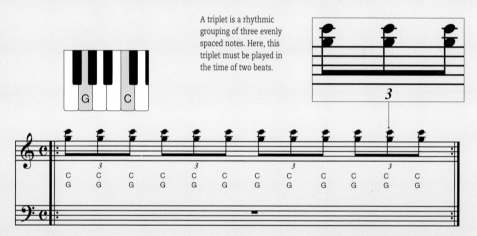

Because this is a triplet figure it will fit with a bass line played with a "swing" rhythm. As you are playing the same notes with your fingers, your wrist can do most of the work here. Practice by holding your arm still, and playing the notes by raising and lowering your wrist. The first note of each triplet has a natural accent so play it slightly louder than the others. This strengthens the rhythm and generates a strong beat.

Mix and match!

All the licks shown on these pages can be played with the previous bass lines. Why not try experimenting with a few different combinations?

Right hand: G–C

Lesson 18:
Boogie-woogie

Step 2

This example is very similar but with an F♯ in the first triplet of each half bar. The F♯ here is the flattened fifth and gives the lick a more "bluesy" sound.

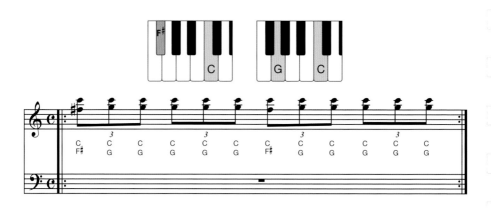

Right hand: F♯–C

Step 3 *track 48*
The next lick is a descending figure based on C chord notes.

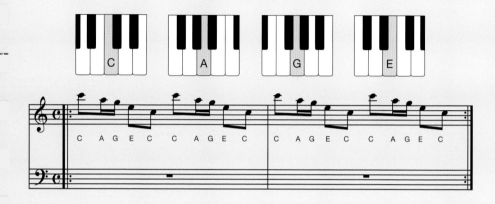

Right hand: **C–C**

Lesson 18:
Boogie-woogie

Step 4

When the progression changes to the F chord, you have to change the E to an
E♭ to make the lick fit the harmony.

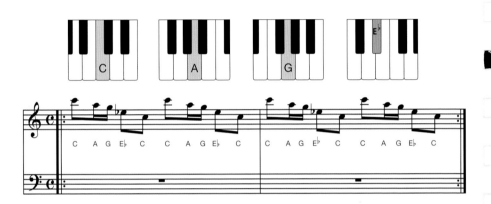

Right hand: C–C

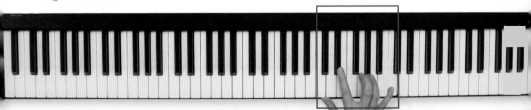

Step 5 *track 49*

The next lick is a triplet pattern.

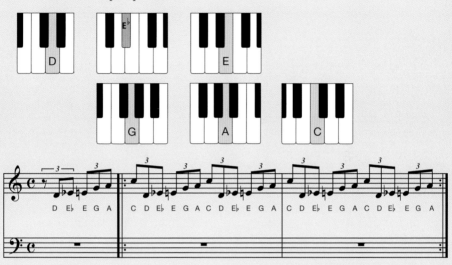

D E♭ E G A | C D E♭ E G A C D E♭ E G A | C D E♭ E G A C D E♭ E G A

Here the D is played with your thumb, the E♭ with your second finger, and then thumb under on the E♮. Then your third, fourth, and fifth fingers should be on the G, A, and C. This requires some patience, so slow it right down and play as evenly as you can.

Because these licks are repetitive, do try and work out your own variations and different ways of linking them together. Also go back to the lessons on the blues scale and blues licks and see if you can combine some of those ideas to create different patterns. The best resource of all is to listen to boogie-woogie pianists and copy what they do—that way you know it's right.

Right hand: **D–C**

19 Rock 'n' roll

From the combined ingredients of rhythm and blues,
gospel, and boogie-woogie, emerged rock 'n' roll,
which became the main driving force behind
virtually all popular music.

Rock 'n' roll history

Several artists can lay a claim to being the inventor of rock 'n' roll, but there is some agreement that the first rock 'n' roll record was "Rocket 88," recorded in 1951 by Jackie Brenston and his Delta Cats (also known as Ike Turner and the Kings of Rhythm—Brenston was credited as he sang lead vocals on this track). Another contender for first ever rock 'n' roll record is "That's All Right Mama," recorded by Elvis Presley in 1954. For fans, it's a contentious issue, but it is widely acknowledged that elements of rock 'n' roll can be traced back as far as the 1920s.

All the early rock 'n' roll records feature a 12-bar blues sequence and boogie-woogie rhythm, with a strong backbeat on the second and fourth beat of each bar. Early rock 'n' roll piano playing takes a lot from boogie-woogie, but the piano's role is to provide accompaniment and fills between the vocal, rather than providing nonstop action as in boogie-woogie. The electric guitar gradually began to take over from the piano in rock 'n' roll groups, and a saxophone or horn section was often used for funky riffs and wailing solos.

Playlist

These songs are some earlier rock 'n' roll recordings, and provide a snapshot of how the style began.

"Rocket 88" **Jackie Brenston and the Deltas**
"That's All Right Mama" **Elvis Presley**
"Rock Around the Clock" **Bill Haley and the Comets**
"Maybellene" **Chuck Berry**
"Pretty Thing" **Bo Diddley**
"Long Tall Sally" **Little Richard**
"Whole Lotta Shakin' Going On" **Jerry Lee Lewis**

Jerry Lee Lewis, a huge American singer, songwriter, and pianist, at the Country Music Festival, Wembley Arena, 1982.

Lesson 19:
Rock 'n' roll

On the CD
Track 50–53
SEE ALSO
Fold-out flap
Lesson 21, *page 108*

Step 1 *track 50*
The first example is a typical rock 'n' roll bass line.

Starting with your left-hand little finger, third finger plays D♯, thumb on E, and then third finger crosses over onto G, second finger on B♭, and thumb on C. There are different fingering possibilities but you do need to cross your thumb over at some point, so this requires some careful practice.

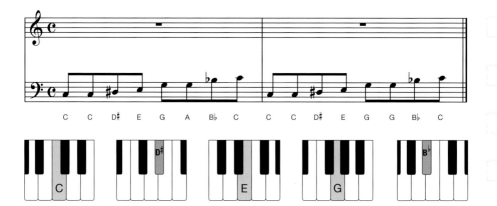

Left hand: C–C

Step 2 *track 51*

This step adds a right-hand chord that is played with every single bass note for a repetitive driving rhythm. Try playing the chord in a higher octave, and the bass line in a lower octave for different effects.

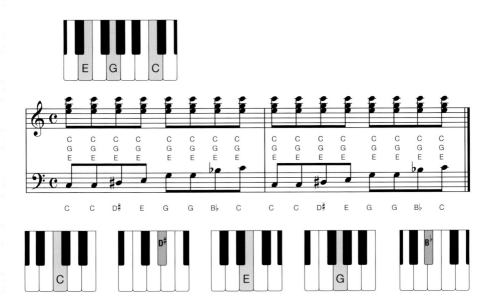

Right hand: E–C
Left hand: C–C

Lesson 19 :
Rock 'n' roll

Step 3 *track 52*

This has the same bass line as the previous steps, but is in the key of F. You can use the same finger pattern as in steps 1 and 2, starting on F. The right hand is playing a riff, which could be used as an introduction or an instrumental section between the vocal parts.

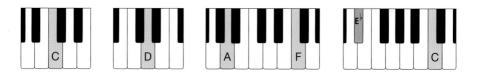

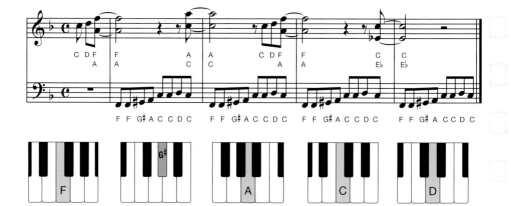

Right hand: E♭–A
Left hand: F–D

Step 4 track 53
This step adds a right-hand chord that is played with every single bass note for a repetitive driving rhythm. Try playing the chord in a higher octave, and the bass line in a lower octave, for different effects.

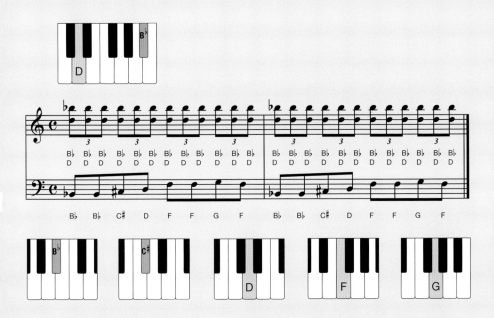

Here, the left-hand bass line is the same, but now in B♭. You can keep the same finger pattern, or it may be easier to start with your fourth finger on the B♭. The right hand plays a triplet rhythm, which is a common type of accompaniment.

These examples are all intended to be played with a "swing" rhythm, as in the boogie-woogie chapter (see page 84), but can also be played with a "straight" feel, which is something that Little Richard pioneered in the mid-1950s.

Right hand: D–B♭ Left hand: B♭–G

20 **Preset heaven**

On the CD
Track 54–59
SEE ALSO
Fold-out flap

Most modern keyboards come with an arsenal of "preset" sounds, which usually includes all orchestral instruments, keyboard and synthesizer voices, a variety of "ethnic" instruments, drums, sound effects, and just about anything else you can think of. Hours of fun can be spent playing a banjo version of the "James Bond" theme, and a rendition of "Love Me Tender" on the bagpipes can be very entertaining, but there are also times when you really want the string preset to sound like the violin section of the New York Philharmonic Orchestra giving it their all on your latest track.

The next few lessons look at how to get the most out of preset voices.

Keyboard preset sounds

All sorts of sounds are available, depending on the keyboard brand.
Here are a few of them:

For serious occasions:	Just for fun:	Rhythms:
• Electric piano	• Percussion	• Rock 1 and 2
• Melodic piano	• Chopsticks on piano	• Swing
• Jazz guitar	• Bells	• Samba
• Strings	• Muted guitar	• Jazz waltz
• Flute	• Funky clavinet raspy	• Disco
• Trumpet	• "Funny fuzz"	• Beguine
• Clarinet	• Synthesized falling effect	• Habanera
• Mandolin	• Cosmic tone	
• Chime	• Space console	
• Harp	• Shimmers	
• Pipe organ	• Dolphins	
• Harpsichord	• Fantasy	
• Jazz-organ-classic	• UFO	
• Chorus: choir sample	• The frog	

Step 1 *track 54*

This example is a guitar preset, which will sound much more like a guitar if you play guitar-type chords:

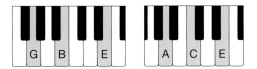

These three chords are typical of the notes in a guitar chord. The first one is just the open strings on a guitar, and the best way to play it is starting from the bottom, holding each note down as you play the next. If you use an "acoustic" or "classical" guitar preset, this should sound very realistic. The next two chords are similar and will also sound very much like a guitar if played from the bottom up.

The keyboard player in a band will often be relied upon to provide all the parts that the bass, guitar, and drums can't cover, the most likely ones being strings, brass, "pads" (see page 116) and sometimes bass lines to fill out the sound.

Right hand: G–E Left hand: E–E

Lesson 20:
Preset heaven

Step 2 *track 55*

This example demonstrates how to make a harp preset sound like a harp. Remember, you have to play something harp-like.

The key signature here is five flats and all the notes in the example are black notes. To get a rough idea of the effect, place your right hand sideways onto a group of black notes and drag it along the black keys, trying to play just one at a time. As you do this, follow your right hand with your left hand, again just on the

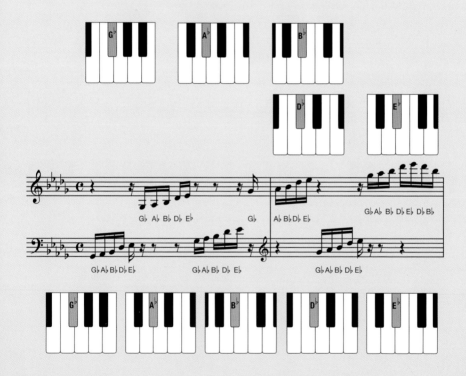

black notes. When you get to the top, change the direction of your hands and come back down. This *glissando* (sliding) technique is much easier on a keyboard than on a piano where the action is much heavier. There are various ways to achieve this effect—you can try just using your thumb or even the back of the hand, but it can hurt if you get it wrong.

Watch out for the changing clef in the left hand!

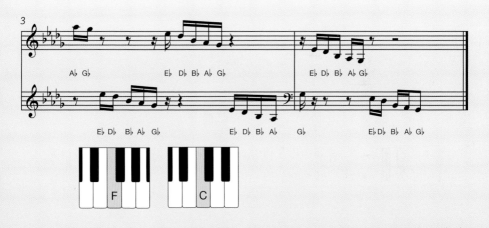

Right hand: G♭–E♭
Left hand: G♭–E♭

21 Bass lines

Playing bass lines on a keyboard means you can do everything that a bass-player does, but with just one hand, leaving your other hand free to play a chord, melody line, or anything else that takes your fancy.

In a band the keyboard player will sometimes "double" the bass line being played by the bass-player, (that is, play exactly the same thing), as a way of strengthening the bass line and giving it more emphasis. Alternatively, if the keyboard player plays the bass line, it frees up the bass-player to do something else, such as doubling a guitar riff or playing a solo. Messing around with bass sounds and bass

Step 1 track 56
This example is the type of bass line found on soul records where the bass is playing a repeated figure, using just three notes.

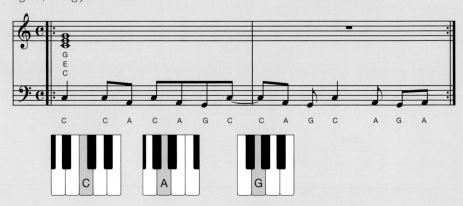

Listen to the CD to get a feel for how the rhythm fits together, and keep practicing over and over until you can play it without really thinking about it. The right-hand chord is a C major root position (see Chord Library, page 160). Add this when you feel confident, and make sure you don't disrupt the flow of the left-hand rhythm.

Right hand: C–G Left hand: G–C

On the CD
Track 56–60

SEE ALSO
Fold-out flap
Chord Library, page 160

lines, is a great way to come up with new ideas for songs. The bass line has to follow the harmony in terms of the chord sequence of the song, and it has to lock in with the rhythmic feel, or groove, of the track. So if you come up with a killer bass line it always provides plenty of inspiration for songwriting.

Many keyboards come with a whole range of different bass presets including acoustic bass, wood bass, electric bass, fingered bass, slap bass, and any number of "synth" bass sounds. Some types of preset work better with a certain type of bass line, so spend time experimenting with the different sounds that you have available.

Step 2 track 57
Many bass lines use octave patterns—this is a way of creating movement when the chords are not moving.

When you play the left-hand part, keep your arm as relaxed as possible. Your wrist should rotate to help the movement between little finger and thumb and you need to be relaxed to do this. The right-hand chord is E minor. It is written right at the start of the measure, but can fit in absolutely anywhere so try moving it around to create different rhythms.

Right hand: E–B Left hand: E–E

Lesson 21:
Bass lines

Step 3 *track 58*
This example is again based on octaves and is a classic disco bass line.

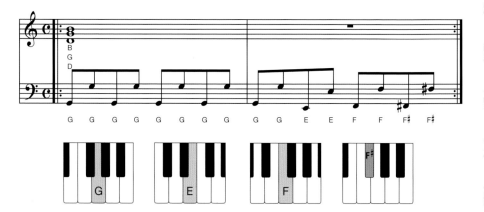

The right-hand chord should fit anywhere in the pattern so try playing it with different bass notes. This would probably work best with "slap bass" or "fingered bass."

Right hand: D–B
Left hand: E –G

Improve your timing

If you have a drum machine or a keyboard that plays auto-accompaniment rhythms, play along to these to improve your timing and feel.

Step 4 *track 59*

Another type of bass line is the "walking" bass line, where the bass plays a steady quarter note rhythm. This style is most associated with jazz but works in many other genres of music as well.

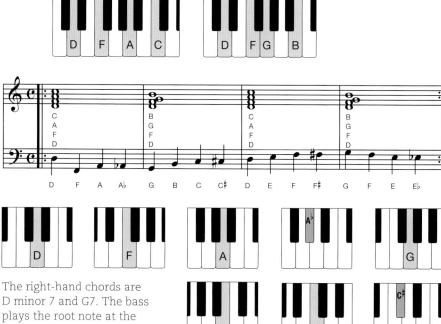

The right-hand chords are D minor 7 and G7. The bass plays the root note at the start of each measure and then uses scale patterns and chromatic passing notes to maintain the walking rhythm. Use "acoustic bass" for this one.

Right hand: **D–C** Left hand: **F–G**

22 String parts

On the CD
Track 60–63

SEE ALSO
Fold-out flap

As a keyboard player in a band, you will often be called upon to impersonate the violin section of an orchestra, and there are several techniques that will help you do this.

Step 1 track 60
A good way of playing chords with a string sound is to use an open "voicing." Voicing means the way in which the notes of a chord are grouped together, so an open voicing means there are larger intervals between the notes in the chord. This example has four chords in an open position:

C major, G major, A minor, E minor

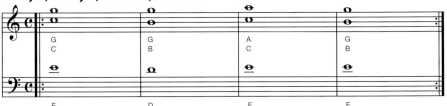

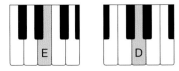

Right hand: B–A
Left hand: D–E

The chords in both steps are C major, G major, A minor, and E minor. If you compare these chords with those in the Chord Library you can see how the same notes are spaced differently to create a different voicing. Play them with a string sound and hear how they

create a feeling of openness and space. Often this is exactly what you are trying to achieve with a string part, and the results can be dramatic when added to the existing instrumentation.

String presets are often divided into "fast strings" and "slow strings" and this refers to the attack of the sound. Slow strings start very quietly and build up gradually, whereas fast strings are louder from the start, for a more aggressive, rhythmical sound. In general, slow strings are better suited to longer notes, and fast strings to quicker, more rhythmic parts. Here, the previous example is adapted to quarter-notes, where the rhythmic elements of the part would sound better with fast strings.

Step 2 *track 61*
Adding this type of part is very effective in marking out different sections in a song. Some string chords can help lift the chorus, or create a different mood.

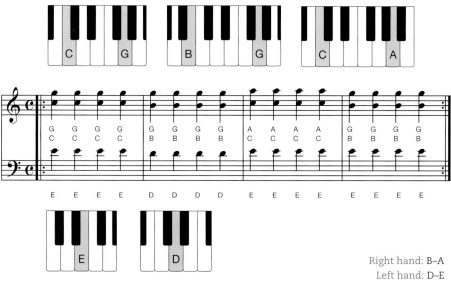

Right hand: B–A
Left hand: D–E

Lesson 22:
String parts

Step 3 *track 62*

Fast scale passages sound very dramatic with a string sound that has a fast attack, or try with a *pizzicato* (plucked) string sound.

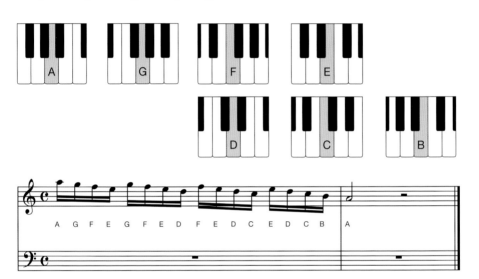

This passage needs to be played neatly and accurately. Start each group of sixteenth-notes with your fourth finger and readjust your hand position in between each. The final A can be played by crossing your third finger over. The next example is a kind of mirror image.

Right hand: **A–A**

Step 4 *track 63*

This time, start each group of sixteenth-notes with your thumb and end with your little finger. Start slowly at first, and gradually build up speed; this is a good exercise for improving your technique.

String parts are excellent for creating atmospheric intros, outros, and "breakdown" sections where the drums drop out, leaving a quieter, more ambient sound.

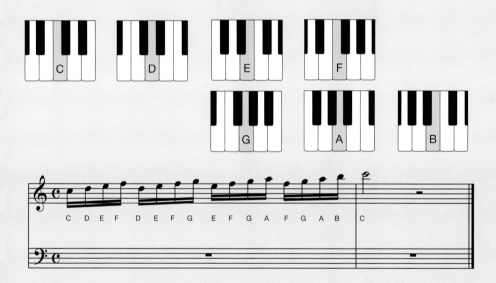

Right hand: C–C

23 *Padding it out*

On the CD
Track 64
SEE ALSO
Fold-out flap
Chord Library, *page 160*

The keyboard "pad" is a sound used to fill a space, or create a background ambience, without intruding too far on the listener's consciousness. It should create some movement and texture but remain in the background. The term "pad" can be used to describe an actual keyboard sound, or the role that a sound is playing in a song, so for example, a string sound can be used as a pad.

Pad presets on modern keyboards can be multilayered voices that create a vast wash of ever-changing and modulating sound with the press of a single key.

These presets are often built up of different components, which give them a dense texture and complexity of sound. Elements of analog synthesizer sounds are often used, with the "filter sweep" being a favorite. This creates an effect where the resonant frequencies of a note sweep up and down, but the fundamental pitch is unchanged. Because pad voices are often very complex you can get away with very simple parts; in fact they almost always have to be simple.

So what you're looking for is a single sustained note that fits with the existing harmony. A good way to approach this is to look for common notes within a chord progression.

Step 1 *track 64*

The chords here are D minor, B♭, and F, which all have an F in them, so a long sustained F will sound effective with a pad sound. This approach doesn't always work as sometimes there are no common notes, but it can be a useful method for finding a way in. You have to rely on your ears as to whether it sounds right or not.

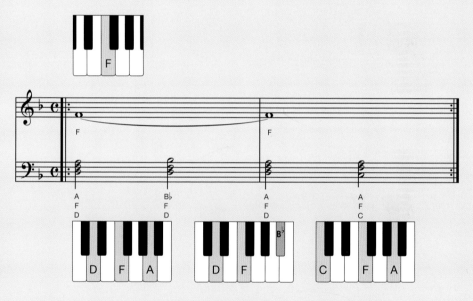

A well-placed single note can be surprisingly effective, and if you're ever struggling to find a useful keyboard part for a song, this approach can be very rewarding.

Right hand: **F**
Left hand: **C–B♭**

24 Brassed off

In the swing bands of the 1930s and 1940s, the brass section provided punchy, aggressive riffs and squealing high notes for sections of real energy and excitement, and piano players would try to emulate this in small group and solo performances, where there was no brass section.

With the advent of synthesizers and samplers, these sounds are easy to reproduce at the press of a button. However, to

Step 1 *track 65*
Soul and rhythm and blues records of the 1960s and 1970s used brass sections of three or four horns, and this example is a unison riff of that type—each horn is playing exactly the same notes. The riff repeats over

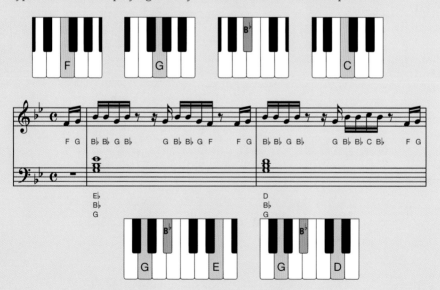

On the CD
Track 65–67

SEE ALSO
Fold-out flap

achieve a convincing effect, you must play notes that correspond authentically to notes that a brass section would play.

Playing brass parts requires special attention to articulation, that is, whether or not the notes are joined together or short and detached. When you play these examples, experiment using very short "stabs," and *legato* (smooth) phrasing.

four measures and there is a different left-hand chord with each measure. This is really to show that a simple riff can fit lots of chords, both major and minor. It is an effective technique to use a repeating riff over changing chords.

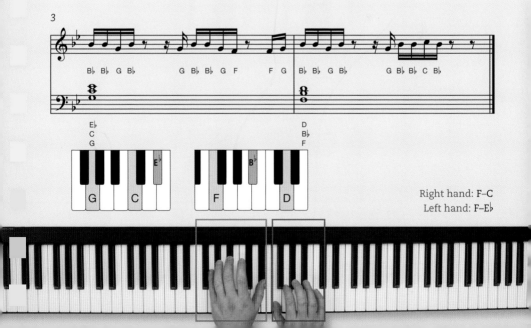

Lesson 24:
Brassed off

Step 2 *track 66*
The next example uses a chord with three notes that would
be played by three separate instruments in a brass section.

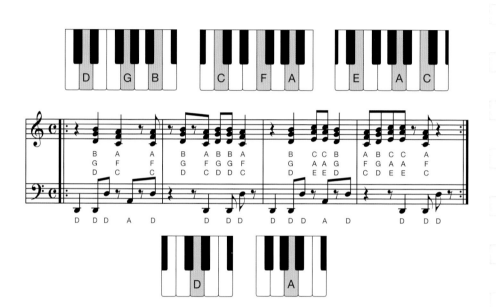

The right-hand part here is made up of triads (three-note chords), that
move around to create melodic and rhythmic interest. The bass line is
in a funk style and is syncopated, that is, with many notes on weak
beats. It is very hard to play with the right-hand part as well, but shows
how the "brass" part fits the style.

Right hand: C–C
Left hand: D–D

Step 3 *track 67*

This example is typical of pop records of the 1980s where "synth brass" took on a life of its own, and was a staple of the grandiose production techniques of the time.

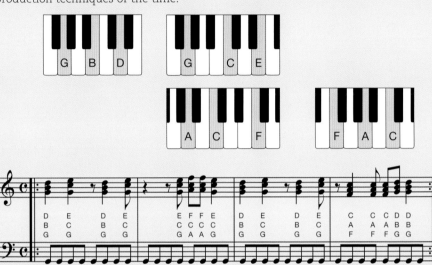

Here the right hand is playing three-note chords, and the bass line is a single repeated note in a rock style that would suit an introduction or middle section to a track.

As a keyboard player you may be expected to come up with brass parts so its useful to have tried experimenting with some. Also, if you are struggling to find a keyboard part for a song or track, try thinking like a horn player instead.

Right hand: F–F Left hand: G

25 *Latin music*

On the CD
Track 68–72

SEE ALSO
Fold-out flap

The music of Cuba, and South and Central America is collectively known as Latin-American, or simply Latin, music. This term covers a vast range of styles from an enormous geographical area but the common features are elements from Spanish song forms, West African rhythms, and European harmonies. Latin music has filtered into all styles of Western music and a knowledge of some of its elements will provide great inspiration for writing and playing.

Latin music is dance music, and the different styles are inextricably linked with their associated dances, for example the Argentinian tango, the Brazilian samba, the Cuban mambo, and the more recent salsa, which originated in New York. More than anything else the rhythmic energy and ingenuity is what distinguishes these styles, and gives Latin music its vibrancy and excitement.

Although the examples on the following pages only scratch the surface of Latin music, they are useful patterns to know for adding a Latin flavor to something else. Having knowledge of different genres and styles will filter through into the music that you really dig.

Playlist

The artists in this playlist are all acknowledged masters, and the chosen tracks are famous recordings, but do check out other tracks by these great musicians.

"Mucho Macho" **Machito and his Afro-Cubans**
"El Watusi" **Ray Barretto**
"The Sun of Latin Music" **Eddie Palmieri**
"Pedro Navaja" **Ruben Blades**
"Dance Mania" **Tito Puente**
"La Camorra" **Astor Piazzola**
"The Composer of 'Desafinado' Plays" **Antonio Carlos Jobim**
"Quarteto Novo" **Hermeto Pascoal**
"Manteca" **Chano Pozo**

Samba

The samba is a high-energy Brazilian style associated with the extravagant street carnivals of Rio de Janeiro, and the traditional form is played by a group of drummers.

The rhythm of the samba has been used to create many crossover styles, such as jazz samba, samba reggae, and bossa nova, where a strong feel of two beats per measure is accompanied by syncopated chord patterns.

Step 1 *track 68*

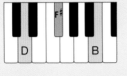

In this example the repeated rhythm of the left hand creates the rhythmic backdrop to the right-hand chord pattern. It may take some practice to maintain a steady pulse in the left hand while playing the right hand chords. As always, practice with hands separately and then very slowly with both hands.

Right hand: D–B Left hand: G–D

Lesson 25:
Latin music

Step 2 *track 69*

This example has the same left-hand rhythm but a more complicated pattern in the right hand.

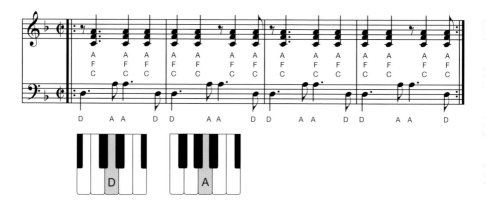

These two examples are typical of samba rhythms being used in a jazz or pop setting. Played more slowly they are typical of bossa nova, which is more relaxed, and uses jazz harmonies to create a mellower, gentler mood.

Right hand: C–A
Left hand: D–A

Mambo *track 70*

Mambo is a dance-form that originated in Cuba in the late 1930s. The rhythm of the dance is characterized by a bass line that doesn't play the first beat of the measure—this can be quite unsettling if you are not used to it.

In this example the left hand plays the first beat of the first measure, but after that the rhythm is more syncopated.

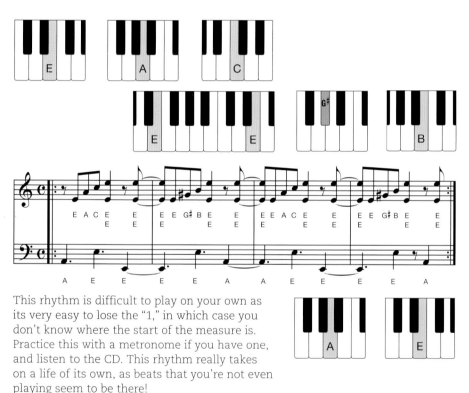

This rhythm is difficult to play on your own as its very easy to lose the "1," in which case you don't know where the start of the measure is. Practice this with a metronome if you have one, and listen to the CD. This rhythm really takes on a life of its own, as beats that you're not even playing seem to be there!

Right hand: E–E
Left hand: E–E

Lesson 25:
Latin music

Salsa

Salsa is a style that originated from various Cuban dance styles in New York in the 1970s. "Salsa" is Spanish for sauce, and the associations are with something hot and spicy, which is what salsa music is all about. The piano has an important role, often playing repeated patterns called "montunos."

Step 1 *track 71*

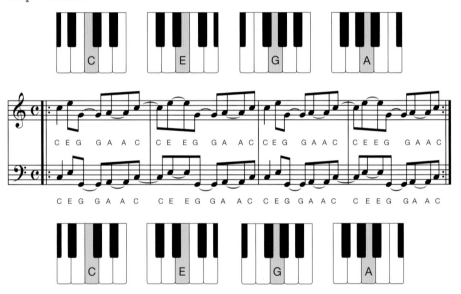

This example has a repeated pattern based on the notes from a C major sixth chord. This is a major chord with the sixth added, which in this case is an A. There are lots of tied notes because of the syncopation, so that only the first note of each 2-bar pattern is on the beat. The right hand and left hand are two octaves apart which creates a big, strong sound on the keyboard.

Right hand: G–E
Left hand: G–E

Step 2 *track 72*

The next montuno has right hand and left hand playing two octaves apart again, but the pattern has more sharps and requires a closer look at the fingering. There are various ways of fingering in this example, but the important thing is to be consistent so that you don't have to think about it when you're playing both hands together. The pattern is based around a G minor chord with added chromatic notes to create movement and tension.

Right hand: B♭–G
Left hand: B♭–G

26 Scale patterns

On the CD
Track 73–80
SEE ALSO
Fold-out flap
Scale Library, *page 210*

Practicing scales is good for technique—it helps to develop finger strength and agility, and it improves your knowledge of different keys—but how can scales be used in music? One way is to practice scale patterns. By rearranging the notes of a scale you can create different patterns, which is great for finding melodic lines to fit with chords.

There are plenty of different fingerings that will work with each of the steps in this lesson, and it is good to experiment with alternatives to keep flexible.

Step 1 *track 73*
For this step, try 1 3 2 4 1 3 2 4 1 3 2 4 3 5 4. The important thing is to turn your thumb under before you run out of fingers, and keep the pulse steady. This scale pattern uses a C major scale:

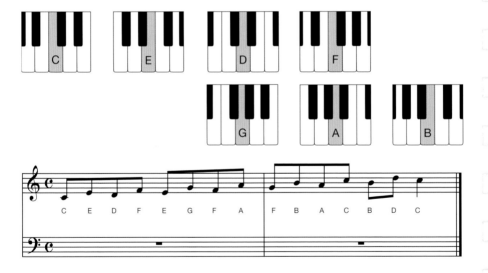

Right hand: C–D

Step 2 *track 74*
Here is another example based on a triplet pattern.

Try 1 2 3 1 2 3 1 2 3 1 2 3 1 2 3 1 2 3 1 2 3 2
or 1 2 3 2 3 4 3 1 2 1 2 3 2 1 2 1 2 3 2 3 4 3.

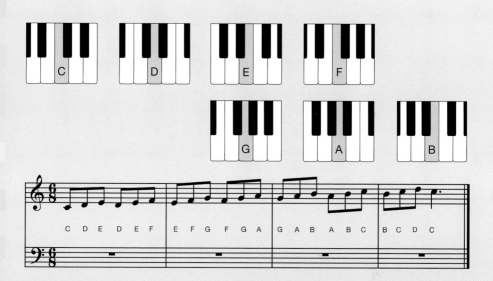

About ⁶⁄₈ time

The ⁶⁄₈ time signature is used to write music that has a triplet beat. Each
bar contains six eighth notes that are usually grouped together in threes,
or triplets, as in the scale pattern examples in this lesson.

Right hand: C–D

Lesson 26:
Scale patterns

Step 3 *track 75*

The examples in steps 1 and 2 can be turned upside down.

Finger numbers to try are:

5 3 4 2 3 1 5 3 4 2 3 1 2 1 2

or 4 2 3 1 4 2 3 1 4 2 3 1 4 2 3

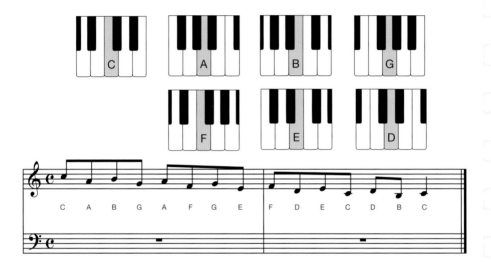

Right hand: B–C

Step 4 *track 76*

Finger numbers to try are:
3 2 1 3 2 1 3 2 1 3 2 1 3 2 1 3 2 1 2
or 5 4 3 4 3 2 3 2 1 5 4 3 4 3 2 3 2 1 3 2 1 2

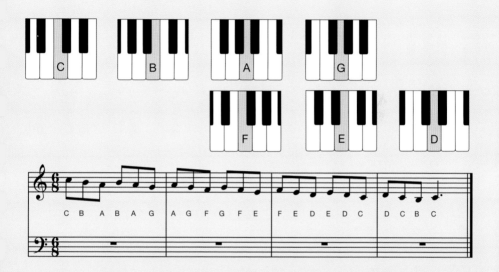

CB A B A G   A G F G F E   F E D E D C   D C B C

Right hand: **B–C**

Lesson 26:
Scale patterns

These are easy to work out in C major because you can see the pattern emerging on the white notes, but it's more difficult in a key with a few sharps or flats.

Step 5 *track 77*
This is the same rhythm as step 1 but in the key of F♯ major:

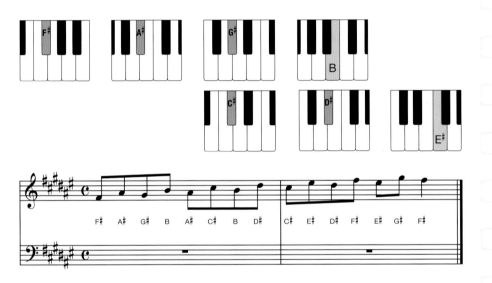

This doesn't look too bad if you ignore the key signature! Refer to the Scale Library (see page 210) to see which notes to use. The E♯ is confusing because it's the same note as F (look at the keyboard below; there isn't a black note to the right of E.) Finger numbers to try are:

1 3 2 4 3 5 1 3 2 4 3 5 1 3 2

Most keyboard players try to avoid keys with this many sharps, but other musicians (guitarists normally) are often oblivious to the difficulties, and you just have to put up with it.

Right hand: F♯–G♯

Step 6 *track 78*
This is the same rhythm as step 2, but in the key
of B♭ major.

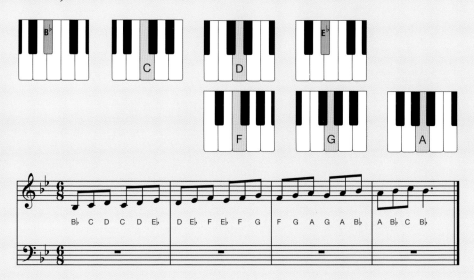

Bb C D C D Eb | D Eb F Eb F G | F G A G A Bb | A Bb C Bb

Finger numbers to try are:
1 2 3 1 2 3 1 2 3 1 2 3 1 2 3 1 2 3 1 2 3 2
or 2 1 2 1 2 3 2 3 1 2 1 2 1 2 3 2 3 4 3 4 5 4.

Right hand: B♭–C

Lesson 26:
Scale patterns

Step 7 *track 79*

The next pattern is in D major which has F♯ and C♯.

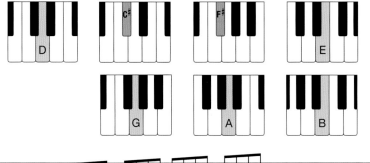

D C♯ D F♯ E D E G   F♯ E F♯ A G F♯ G B   A G A C♯ B A B D   C♯ B C♯ E D

Again, look at the Scale Library to see the notes of the scale (see page 210), and then practice the pattern, making sure you have the correct black notes.

Finger numbers to try are:
2 1 2 4 3 2 3 5 3 2 3 5 3 2 3 5 2 1 2 4 3 2 3 5 3 2 3 5 4.

Right hand: C♯–E

Step 8 *track 80*

Here is the descending version of the same pattern, this time in E major, which has F♯, C♯, G♯, and D♯.

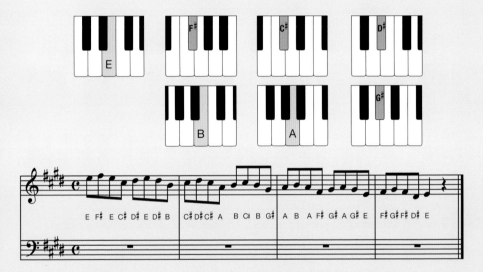

E F♯ E C♯ D♯ E D♯ B | C♯ D♯ C♯ A | B C♯ B G♯ | A B A F♯ G♯ A G♯ E | F♯ G♯ F♯ D♯ E

Finger numbers to try are:

4 5 4 2 3 4 3 1 4 5 4 2 3 4 3 2 4 5 4 2 3 4 3 1 4 5 4 2 3.

There are endless variations of these types of patterns so try inventing some of your own. In lesson 27 we will look at how scale patterns can fit different chord progressions and how they can help with improvising and soloing.

Right hand: D♯–F♯

27 Common chord progressions

On the CD
Track 81–86

SEE ALSO
Fold-out flap
Chord Library, page 160

There is such a bewildering array of different styles with only subtle differences to identify them, that it is often easier to see what they have in common. In many cases it is the harmonic structure, or chord progression.

Step 1 track 81
This extract shows the harmonic sequence that underpins a piece written by Johann Pachelbel in 1680. All of the chords come from the key of D major, which means that it is diatonic—that is, there are no accidentals.

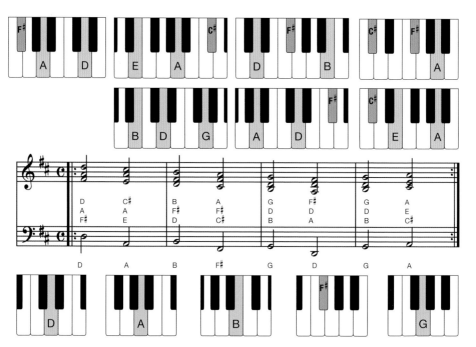

Right hand: **A–D** Left hand: **D–D**

Step 2 *track 82*
The next example is in the key of F, so watch the B♭:

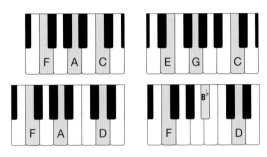

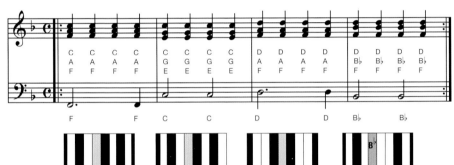

Right hand: E–D
Left hand: F–D

Lesson 27:
Common chord progressions

Step 3 *track 83*

The next chord sequence has a chord that is chromatic—that is, it contains notes that do not belong to the key, which is why there is an accidental in the music. This chord provides extra "color" and movement.

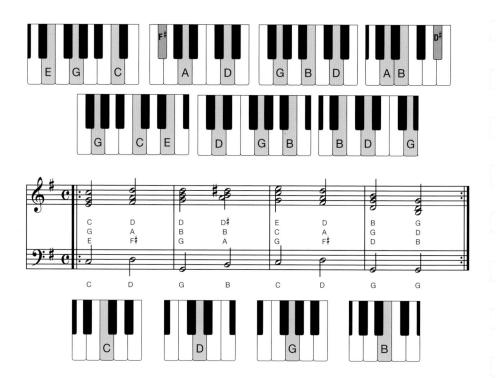

Right hand: B–E
Left hand: G–D

Step 4 *track 84*

Here are some more chord progressions. Remember to practice them with different patterns and at different speeds.

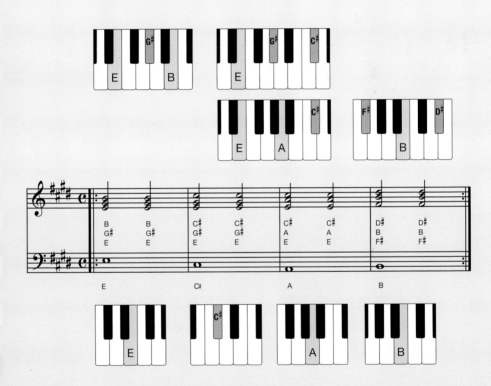

Right hand: E–D♯
Left hand: A–E

Lesson 27:
Common chord progressions

Extending chord progressions

To get the most from this section you need to apply these chord progressions to the different comping patterns in Lessons 7 and 12. Doing this will help you really get to know the keyboard and will force you to work out exactly what is happening with the chords. Another "extension" of this is to transpose the examples into different keys. If you take four different chord progressions, four different comping patterns, and play them in all twelve keys, that gives you 182 exercises to practice—so get busy!

Step 5 *track 85*

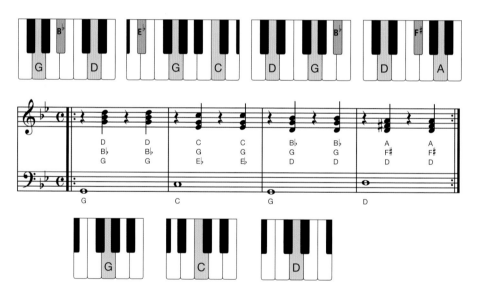

Right hand: D–D Left hand: G–D

Step 6 *track 86*

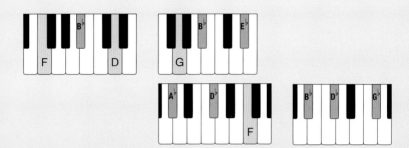

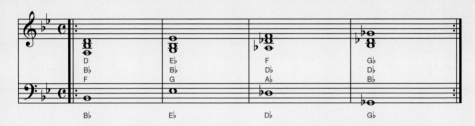

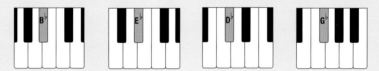

D
Bb
F

Eb
Bb
G

F
Db
Ab

Gb
Db
Bb

Bb

Eb

Db

Gb

Right hand: F–Gb
Left hand: Gb–Eb

28 Improvising on chords

On the CD
Track 87–91
SEE ALSO
Fold-out flap
Lesson 26, page 128

"Let's have a keyboard solo after the second verse!"
It's a great idea, but what do you play? Your
starting point has to be the chord sequence that
the solo is going to fit over; it could be the same
chords as the verse, or the chorus, or an entirely new section.

Step 1 *track 87*

This example uses chords that all come from the key of D major, which means that any notes from D major should fit. The music shows how a scale pattern (see page 128), can be used to create a melodic line.

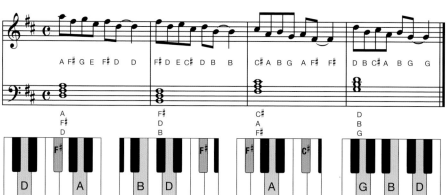

Right hand: F#–A Left hand: B–D

Step 2 *track 88*

The pattern becomes a bit predictable so try changing the last two measures.

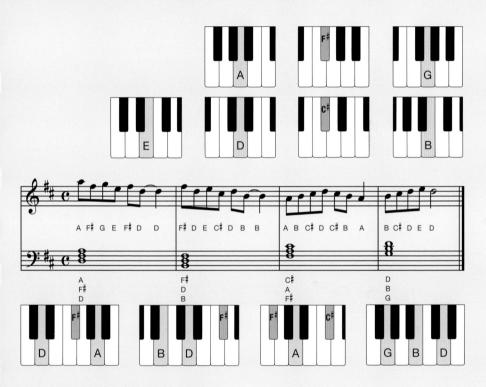

A F# G E F# D   D

F# D E C# D B   B

A B C# D C# B   A

B C# D E   D

The third and fourth measures are going up and down the scale, still just using notes from the D major scale.

Right hand: A–A
Left hand: B–D

Lesson 28:
Improvising on chords

There are several points to bear in mind when considering the art of improvising.

It is a big advantage to have a good knowledge of scales and keys, so that you can choose the correct scale to fit over a given chord sequence. This is something that develops over time and with experience.

Very often in solos "less is more"—one or two simple ideas can often be much more effective than a whole load of notes played at high speed—although sometimes a whole load of notes played at high speed is exactly what you want.

Rules are made to be broken, and if you fancy playing a C minor scale over an F♯ minor chord then do so—it might sound amazing!

Step 3 *track 89*
You can develop step 2 further by changing the rhythm.

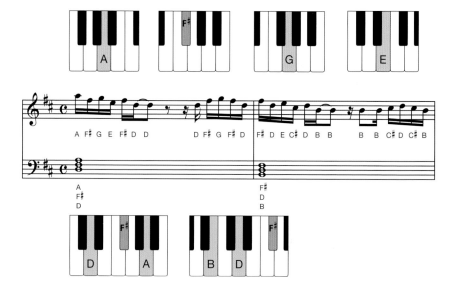

Here the speed of the phrases is doubled by changing them to sixteenth-notes and then some more scale pattern ideas were added in the gaps. This gets quite complicated but comes from developing very simple ideas from one scale.

Improvising as composing

Many a great song has been written as a result of a "jam"; a loose, improvised playing session where ideas flow and mistakes don't matter. Having the confidence to play without needing written music is very liberating, and is often the first step toward writing your own music.

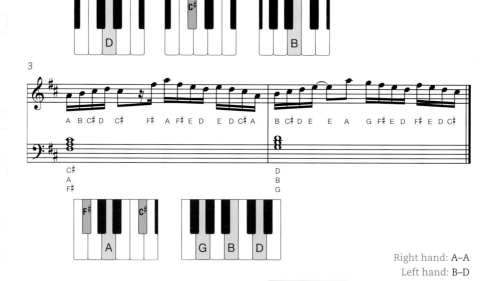

Right hand: A–A
Left hand: B–D

Lesson 28:
Improvising on chords

Step 4 *track 90*

This example has a 4-bar sequence in G minor with the chords
G minor, B♭, E♭, and D7. The right hand plays a three-note phrase
that repeats over each chord change.

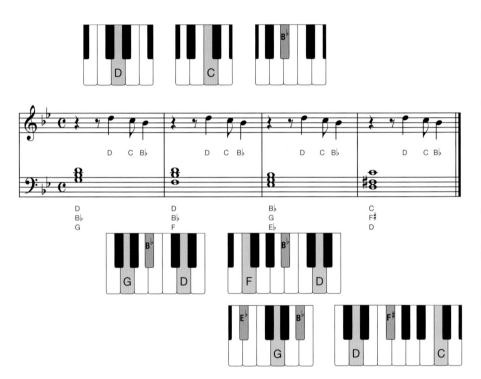

Repeating a simple melody over changing chords can sound very effective and be a
useful starting point for a solo. You could also try keeping the melodic repetition,
but altering the rhythm each time.

Right hand: B♭–D
Left hand: D–D

Step 5 *track 91*

Another approach is to repeat the rhythm of the melody but change the actual notes. The chords are all in the key of G minor so choose melody notes from that scale. The final F♯ here is not in the key signature, but is in the harmonic minor scale (check the Scale Library if you're not clear about this, see page 210).

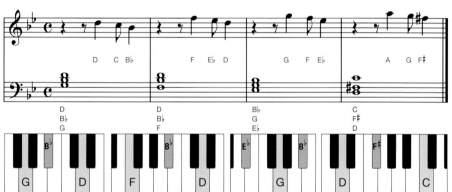

Repetition and variation

A technique that is easy to overlook is repetition. If something you play sounds good, why not play it again? Or play it again but change it slightly.

Right hand: B♭–A Left hand: D–D

29 *Jazzing it up*

Love or loathe the syncopated rhythms, the strong expressions of emotion, and the sometimes deliberately distorted pitch; jazz is impossible to ignore. The influence of jazz on all Western music is enormous. As an aspiring keyboard player, a few jazz chords and a basic knowledge of improvising techniques will go a long way.

Jazz history

There is no real agreement about where the word "jazz" originally comes from, but the origins of the music itself are clearer. Early styles such as Dixieland emerged from a mixture of blues and ragtime in the southern States, particularly around New Orleans, and gradually spread north toward Chicago in the 1920s. In the 1930s and 1940s, big bands ruled supreme with Count Basie, Duke Ellington, and Benny Goodman the big names of the swing era. As the big band craze died down, smaller groups became popular, with the bebop innovations of Charlie Parker and Dizzy Gillespie taking jazz forward.

Throughout the 1950s and 1960s, jazz diversified into many different forms, as free—or avant-garde—jazz and modal jazz converged with European avant-garde classical music, while jazz fusion leant more on the rock and funk of the late 1960s and 1970s.

This rapid evolution makes a definition of jazz almost impossible to pin down but certain features are more or less constant. The use of the blues runs through most jazz, whether the actual 12-bar form, or the use of blues inflection and tonality. Another essential feature is improvisation, as no two jazz performances are the same.

Playlist

Here are some of the most influential jazz pianists with suggested listening, rather than specific tracks.

James P Johnson "Carolina Shout" is his most famous recording.

Fats Waller Many outstanding recordings, either solo piano or with groups.

Teddy Wilson Solo piano and recordings with

Benny Goodman.

Bud Powell Some of his finest recordings were with **Charlie Parker**.

McCoy Tyner Albums with the **John Coltrane Quartet** in the 1960s.

Wynton Kelly "Kind of Blue" by **Miles Davis**.

Herbie Hancock "Headhunters."

Keith Jarrett "Standards Vol 1" and "Standards Vol 2."

Chick Corea "Now He Sings Now He Sobs."

Duke Ellington, composer and band leader, in 1966.
One of the most influential figures in jazz.

Lesson 29:
Jazzing it up

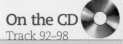

On the CD
Track 92–98
SEE ALSO
Fold-out flap
Chord Library, page 160

Major Chords

The major chord is made up of the root, the third, and the fifth notes of the scale. Notes that can be added are the sixth, the seventh, and the ninth.

Step 1 *track 92*

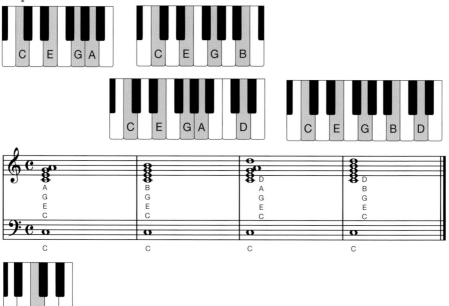

These four chords are C major with an added sixth, added seventh, sixth and ninth, and seventh and ninth. Building the chords from the bottom up is the easiest way to understand which notes are being used, but not necessarily the best way to play the chords. If you are playing the root note with your left hand, then it can be left out of the right-hand chord, which becomes a "rootless" voicing.

Right hand: **C–D** Left hand: **C**

Step 2 *track 93*
If you take the last two chords from Step 1, leave out the root note (in this case C), and invert them by rearranging the notes, you get a chord that is easier to play and sounds better.

This is called a "closed voicing," and because the notes are close together they are quite difficult to read, so take your time to get it right.

Jazz harmony

Jazz music has developed a harmonic language all of its own, although derived mainly from Western classical music, and it is richer and more complex than the harmony of other folk or popular music. The basic ingredient is the addition of chord extensions, which are notes that are added to the main chord types.

Right hand: A–G Left hand: C

Lesson 29:
Jazzing it up

Minor chords

You can apply the same method to a minor triad (three-note chord), by adding a sixth, seventh, and ninth.

Step 3 *track 94*

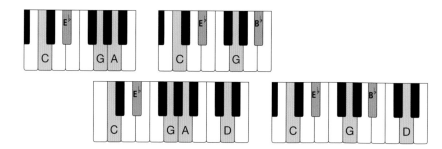

Right hand: C–D
Left hand: C

Step 4 *track 95*

Again, by omitting the root note, and rearranging the remaining notes, the chord is rendered much more playable.

Right hand: **A–G**
Left hand: **C**

Lesson 29:
Jazzing it up

Dominant seventh chords

Dominant seventh chords provide more potential for adding different chord extensions, as they are more transitional, and less stable, than major and minor chords. The notes that you have added to the major and minor chords can also be added to dominant seventh chords.

Step 5 *track 96*

These chords are C7 with an added ninth and thirteenth.

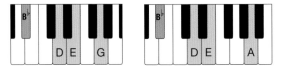

G
E
D
B♭

A
E
D
B♭

C

C

Right hand: B♭–A
Left hand: C

Step 6 *track 97*

The added notes can be sharpened or flattened to create a whole array of different dominant seventh chords. Here are a few possibilities:

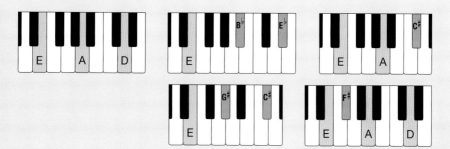

In these examples, the left hand plays the root note as well as the seventh to free up the right hand to play more chord extensions.

These chords still function as dominant chords, which means that they can all resolve to an F major, or F minor chord. They can also function as the first chord in a blues-type progression.

Right hand: E–E♭
Left hand: C–B♭

Lesson 29:
Jazzing it up

Step 7 *track 98*

This example is a short piece using some jazz chords. Here, the left hand plays a root note while the right hand plays a melody line over the top.

This lesson has taken a brief look at the use of chord extensions to create jazz chords. There are many other elements to playing jazz, such as learning jazz repertoire and jazz improvisation techniques, but the use of jazz chords is a good way to introduce a jazz sound to your playing. Experimenting with different chord extensions and inversions can be a fantastic springboard for writing tunes, and for finding different sounds that you might not otherwise come across.

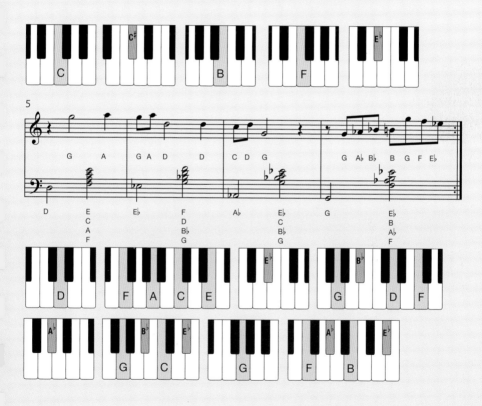

Right hand: G–B♭ Left hand: F–G

30 *Playing in a band*

After hours of lonely practice in your bedroom it's time to get out and make some noise, and the best way to do it is by playing in a band. Playing music with other people is one of the most rewarding aspects of learning an instrument, so consider joining a band once you have some confidence.

There are two routes to follow—either join a band that needs a keyboard player or start a band yourself.

Join a band

The first option involves checking local papers, music press, and music store noticeboards to find a band that needs a keyboard player. Bands essentially fall into two categories: original bands and cover bands. If you want to gain experience fast and earn some cash while you do it, opt for the latter, as cover bands are likely to be semi-pro outfits and will, in general, gig more frequently than original bands. Cover bands usually play a mixture of musical genres unless they are a tribute band dedicated to playing only one group's material.

After making contact you may be required to audition. You're going to be nervous, but just give it your best shot. Use this handy checklist to make sure you don't leave anything to chance.

The Audition

1 Find out about the band

Write a list of questions before you get in contact. How long have they been together? How many gigs do they do? What areas do they play in? How much money do they earn on average per gig? Where do they rehearse (and will this cost you money)? What are the gigs like?

2 Find out what you will be expected to play

If this is the band you really want to join, learn a couple of songs before the audition. And don't forget to check what key they play them in (bands will often change songs from the original key to suit a singer's voice).

3 Ask what you will need at the audition

Find out if you need to take your own gear, or if there will be a keyboard amp there you can use. Take your own keyboard even if you don't have to—there's nothing worse than trying to play on a strange instrument when you're nervous!

Start your own band

The second option is to start your own band. This is a trickier proposition although if you have friends who are learning instruments as well, this can be the way forward. The advantages are that you can choose the material yourself, and if you have written some songs, this is the ideal way to get them heard. The more people in a band, the more difficult it is to organize rehearsals, so start small, and build it up. If you know a bass player or guitarist, the ideal thing to do is to learn songs together, and then recruit other members when you know what you're doing.

Tim Rice-Oxley from
Keane, a hugely successful
British piano-rock band.

4 Be early

If you can't turn up on time for the audition you probably won't turn up on time for gigs either. It doesn't matter how good you are—if you stumble in late you're unlikely to get the gig.

5 Be aware of your volume

If you play too loudly or too quietly you are not gong to sound convincing or effective. If you're using a hired amp, familiarize yourself with the controls before you start and don't be afraid to change the settings mid-song—this is a perfectly acceptable thing to do.

6 Look the part

Every band has some kind of image. Do your homework and fit in!

The advantage of joining an existing band is that a lot of the work has already been done—you just have to slot in. With any luck, before you know it, you'll be gigging, gaining experience, and earning some cash.

Chord
Library

This comprehensive section
provides the notation, and
diagrams, for all the major and
harmonic minor chords. Root,
1st, and 2nd inversions are
included for right and left hands.

Left hand

C major

Root position

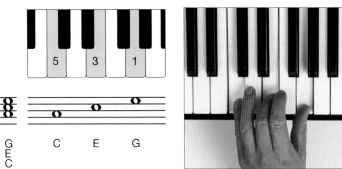

G
E
C   C   E   G

1st inversion

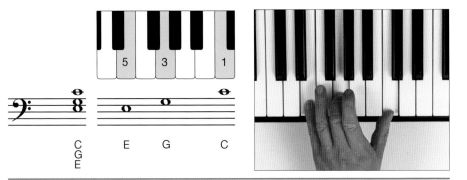

C
G
E   E   G   C

2nd inversion

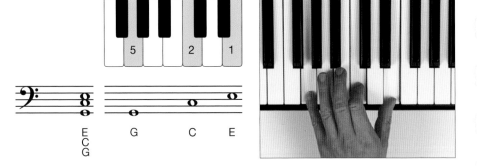

E
C
G   G   C   E

C major

Root position

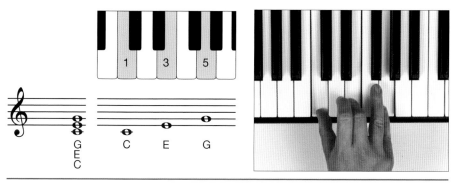

G
E
C

C   E   G

1st inversion

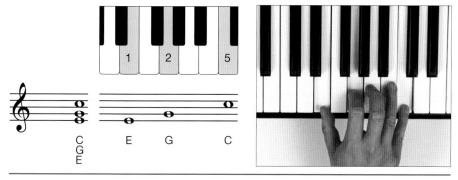

C
G
E

E   G   C

2nd inversion

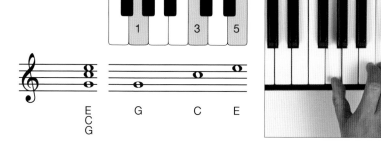

E
C
G

G   C   E

G major

Root position

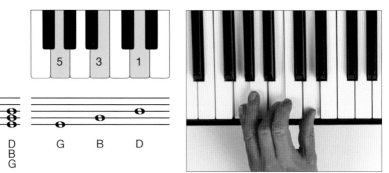

D
B
G

G   B   D

1st inversion

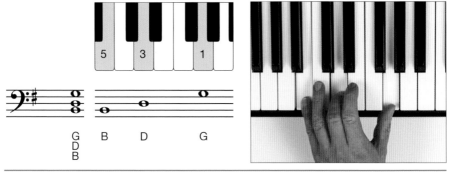

G
D
B

B   D   G

2nd inversion

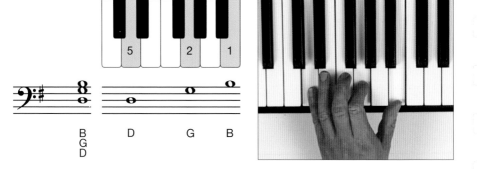

B
G
D

D   G   B

G major

Root position

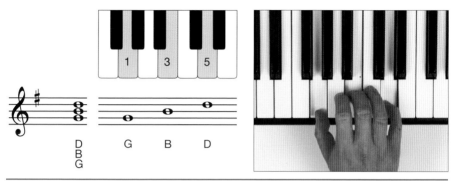

D
B
G

G   B   D

1st inversion

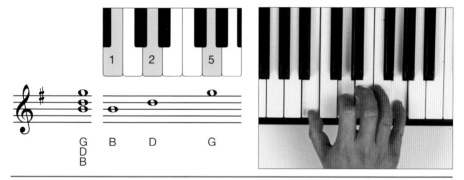

G
D
B

B   D   G

2nd inversion

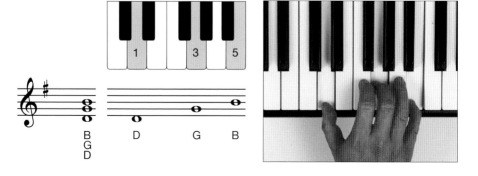

B
G
D

D   G   B

Left hand — **D major**

Root position

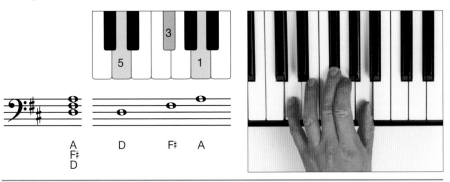

A
F#
D

D F# A

1st inversion

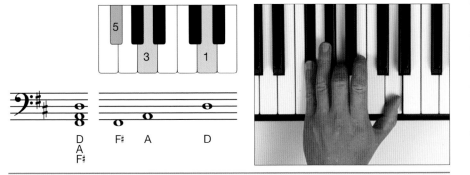

D
A
F#

F# A D

2nd inversion

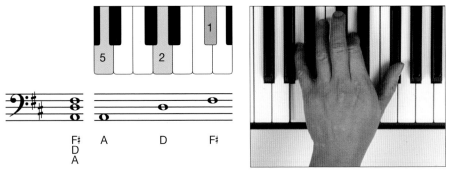

F#
D
A

A D F#

D major

Root position

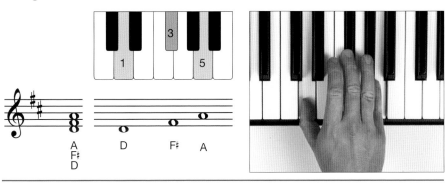

A
F#
D

D   F#   A

1st inversion

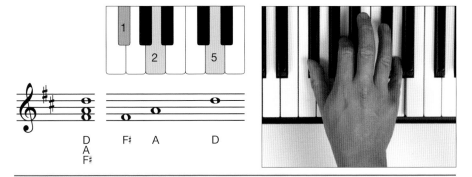

D
A
F#

F#   A   D

2nd inversion

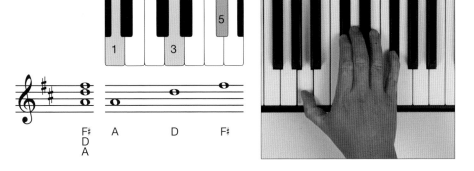

F#
D
A

A   D   F#

Left hand

A major

Root position

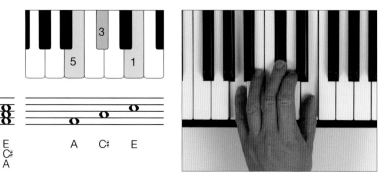

E
C♯
A

A   C♯   E

1st inversion

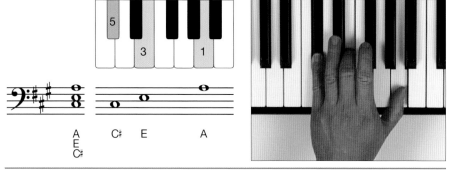

A
E
C♯

C♯   E   A

2nd inversion

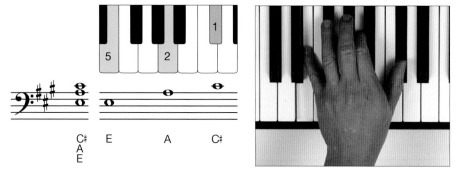

C♯
A
E

E   A   C♯

A major

Root position

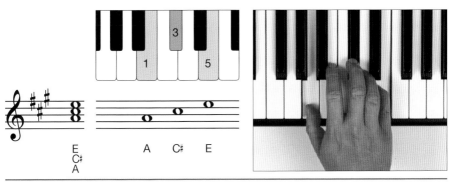

E
C#
A

A   C#   E

1st inversion

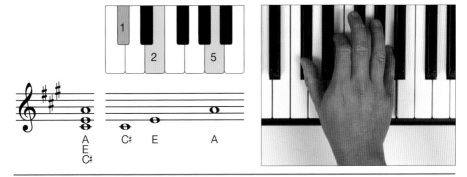

A
E
C#

C#   E   A

2nd inversion

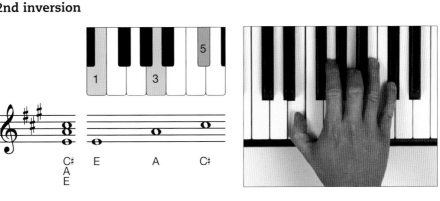

C#
A
E

E   A   C#

E major

Root position

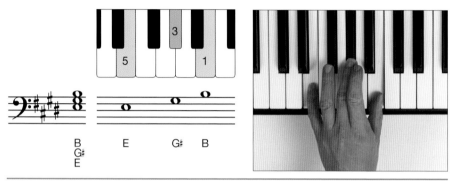

B
G♯
E

E G♯ B

1st inversion

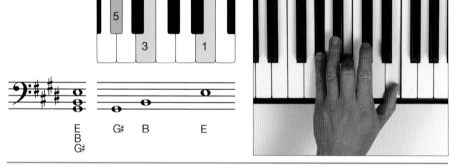

E
B
G♯

G♯ B E

2nd inversion

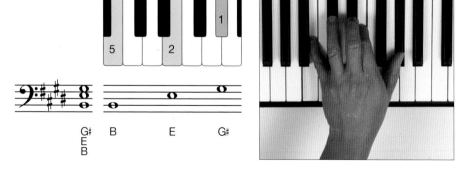

G♯
E
B

B E G♯

E major

Root position

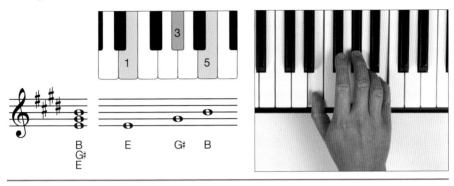

B
G#
E

E   G#   B

1st inversion

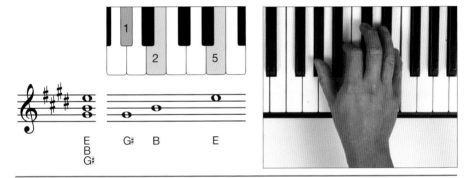

E
B
G#

G#   B   E

2nd inversion

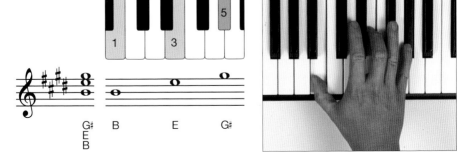

G#
E
B

B   E   G#

Left hand

B major

Root position

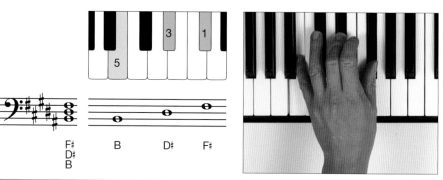

F♯
D♯
B

B D♯ F♯

1st inversion

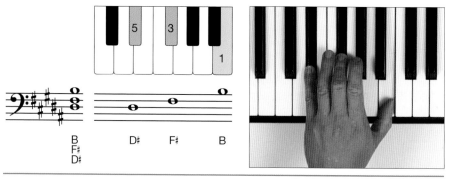

B
F♯
D♯

D♯ F♯ B

2nd inversion

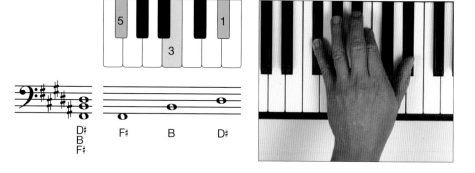

D♯
B
F♯

F♯ B D♯

B major

Root position

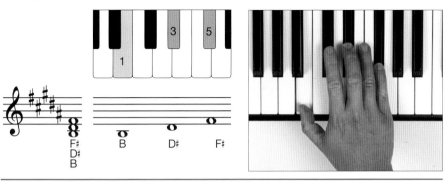

F#
D#
B

B   D#   F#

1st inversion

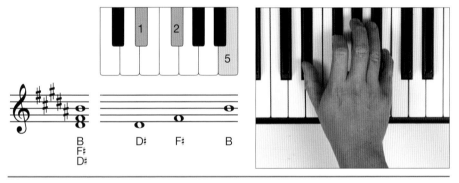

B
F#
D#

D#   F#   B

2nd inversion

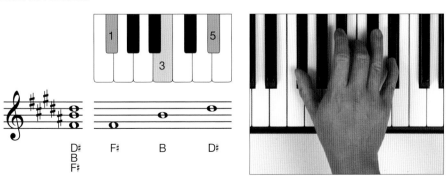

D#
B
F#

F#   B   D#

Left hand — G flat major (also known as F sharp major)

Root position

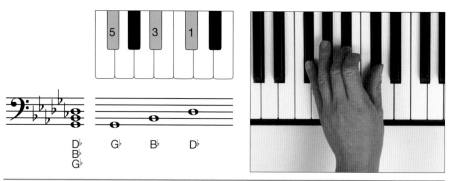

D♭
B♭
G♭
   G♭   B♭   D♭

1st inversion

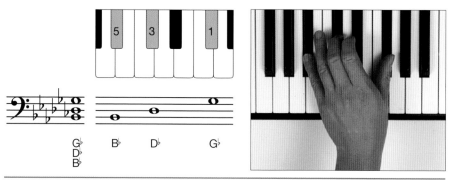

G♭
D♭
B♭
   B♭   D♭   G♭

2nd inversion

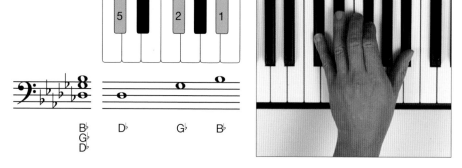

B♭
G♭
D♭
   D♭   G♭   B♭

G flat major Right hand

Root position

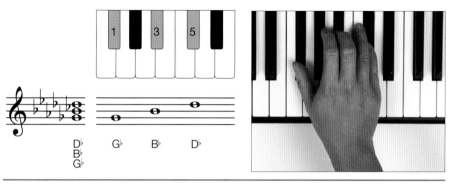

D♭
B♭
G♭

G♭   B♭   D♭

1st inversion

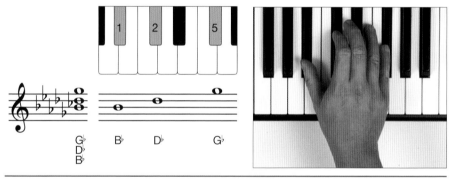

G♭
D♭
B♭

B♭   D♭   G♭

2nd inversion

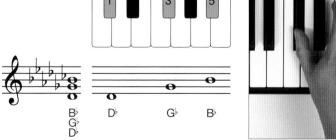

B♭
G♭
D♭

D♭   G♭   B♭

D flat major

Root position

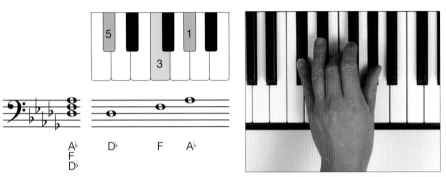

A♭
F
D♭

D♭   F   A♭

1st inversion

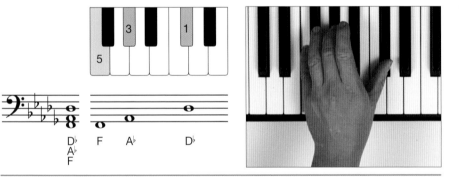

D♭
A♭
F

F   A♭   D♭

2nd inversion

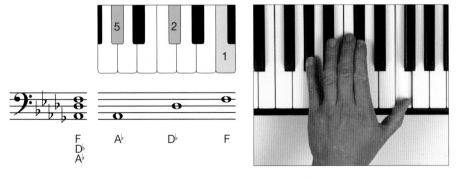

F
D♭
A♭

A♭   D♭   F

D flat major

Root position

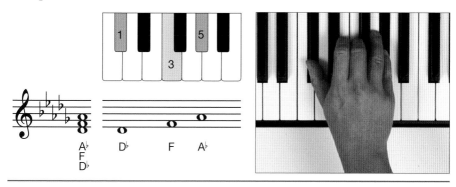

A♭
F
D♭

D♭   F   A♭

1st inversion

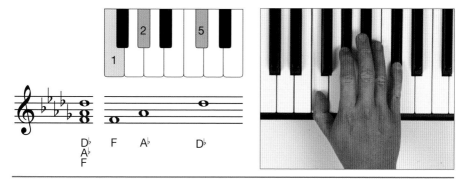

D♭
A♭
F

F   A♭   D♭

2nd inversion

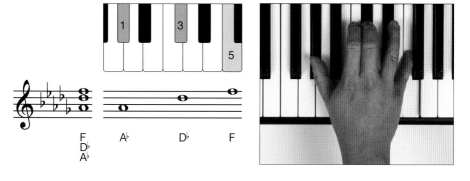

F
D♭
A♭

A♭   D♭   F

Left hand

A flat major

Root position

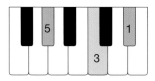

E♭
C
A♭

A♭   C   E♭

1st inversion

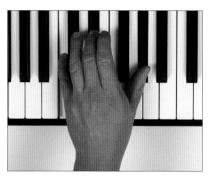

A♭
E♭
C

C   E♭   A♭

2nd inversion

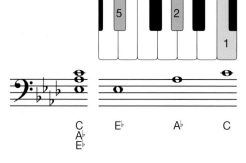

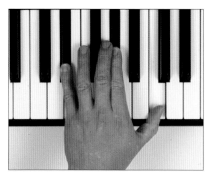

C
A♭
E♭

E♭   A♭   C

A flat major   Right hand

Root position

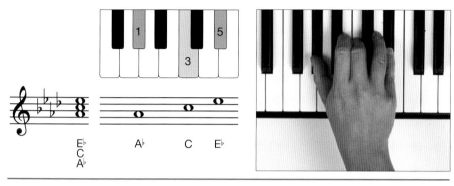

E♭
C
A♭

A♭   C   E♭

1st inversion

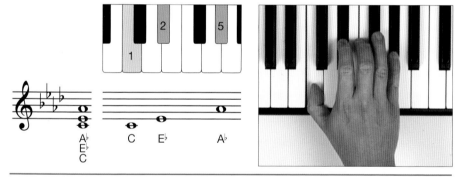

A♭
E♭
C

C   E♭   A♭

2nd inversion

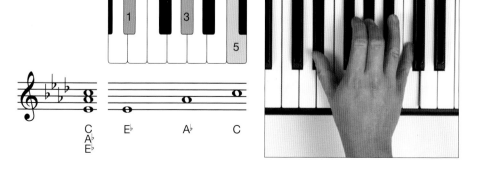

C
A♭
E♭

E♭   A♭   C

E flat major

Root position

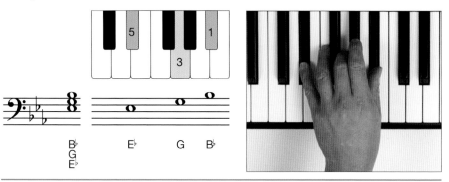

B♭
G
E♭

E♭   G   B♭

1st inversion

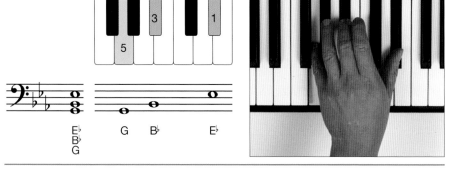

E♭
B♭
G

G   B♭   E♭

2nd inversion

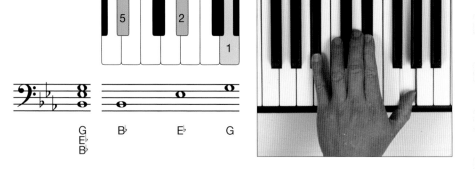

G
E♭
B♭

B♭   E♭   G

E flat major

Root position

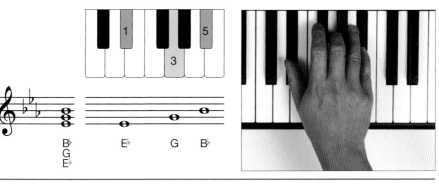

B♭
G
E♭

E♭   G   B♭

1st inversion

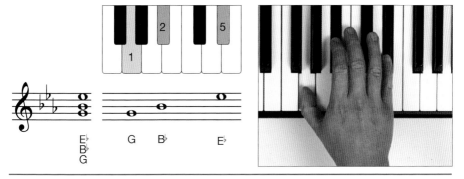

E♭
B♭
G

G   B♭   E♭

2nd inversion

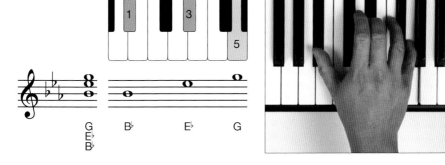

G
E♭
B♭

B♭   E♭   G

Left hand # B flat major

Root position

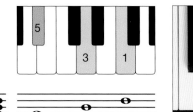

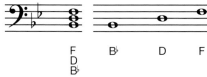

F
D
B♭

B♭   D   F

1st inversion

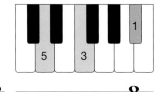

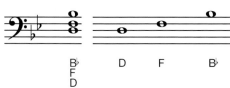

B♭
F
D

D   F   B♭

2nd inversion

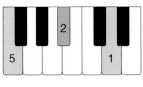

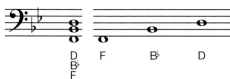

D
B♭
F

F   B♭   D

B flat major

Root position

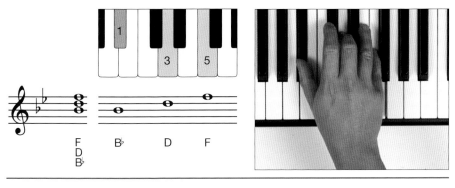

F
D
B♭

B♭   D   F

1st inversion

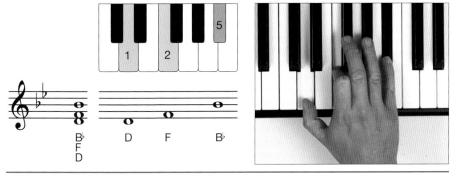

B♭
F
D

D   F   B♭

2nd inversion

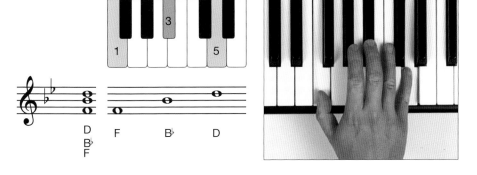

D
B♭
F

F   B♭   D

F major

Root position

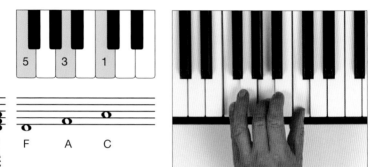

F
A
C
 F   A   C

1st inversion

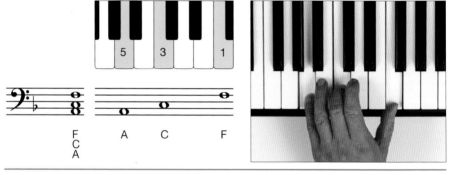

F
C
A
 A   C   F

2nd inversion

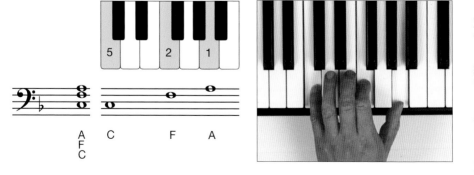

A
F
C
 C   F   A

F major Right hand

Root position

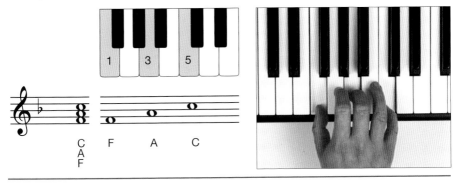

C
A
F

F   A   C

1st inversion

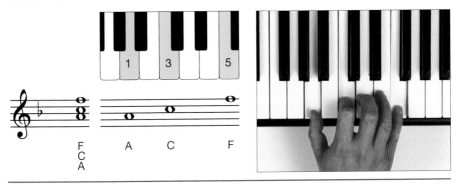

F
C
A

A   C   F

2nd inversion

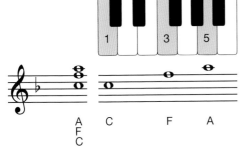

A
F
C

C   F   A

A minor

Root position

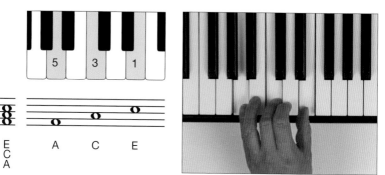

E
C
A

A   C   E

1st inversion

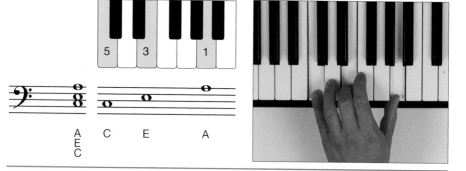

A
E
C

C   E   A

2nd inversion

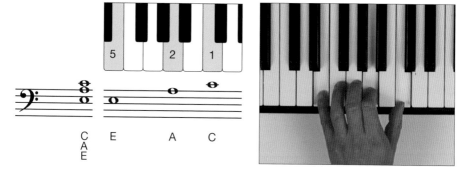

C
A
E

E   A   C

A minor
Right hand

Root position

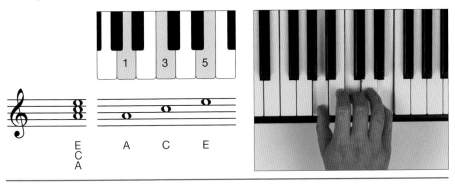

E
C
A

A   C   E

1st inversion

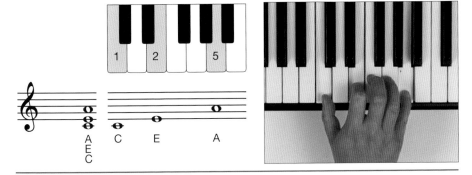

A
E
C

C   E   A

2nd inversion

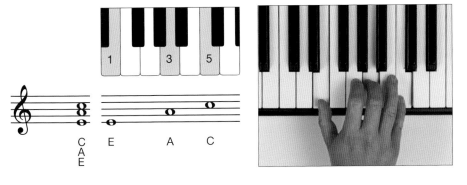

C
A
E

E   A   C

Left hand ## E minor

Root position

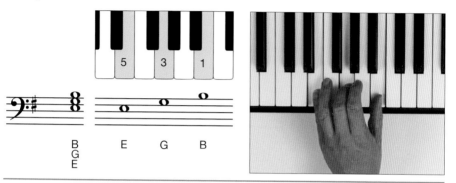

5   3   1

B
G
E   E   G   B

1st inversion

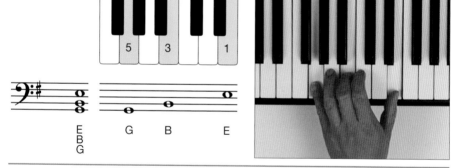

5   3   1

E
B
G   G   B   E

2nd inversion

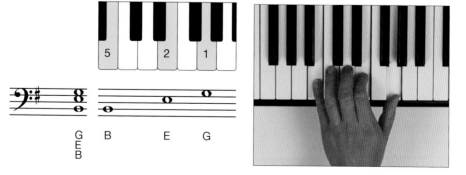

5   2   1

G
E
B   B   E   G

E minor

Root position

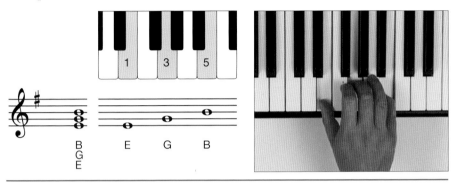

B
G
E

E   G   B

1st inversion

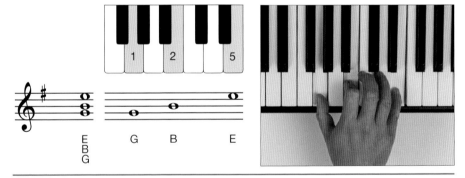

E
B
G

G   B   E

2nd inversion

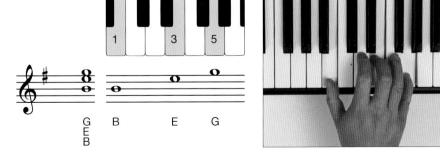

G
E
B

B   E   G

B minor

Root position

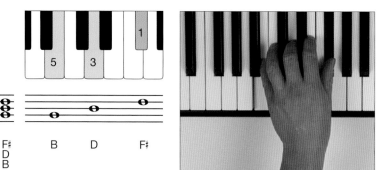

F♯
D
B

B D F♯

1st inversion

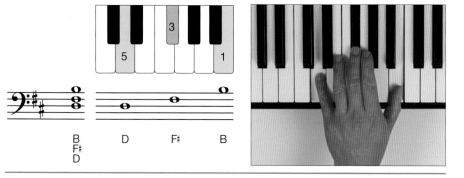

B
F♯
D

D F♯ B

2nd inversion

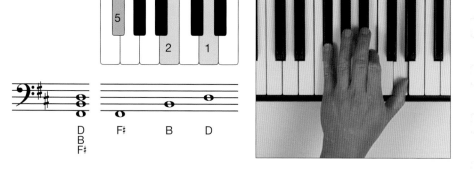

D
B
F♯

F♯ B D

B minor

Root position

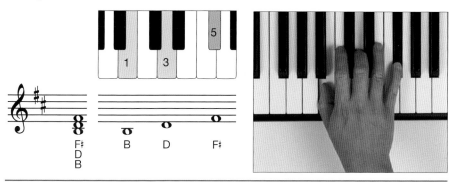

F#
D
B

B   D   F#

1st inversion

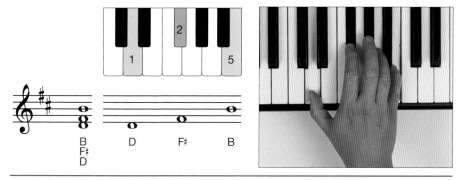

B
F#
D

D   F#   B

2nd inversion

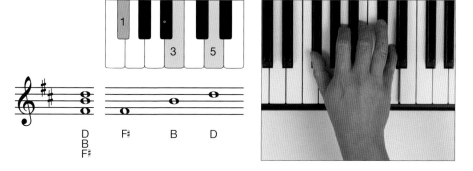

D
B
F#

F#   B   D

F sharp minor

Root position

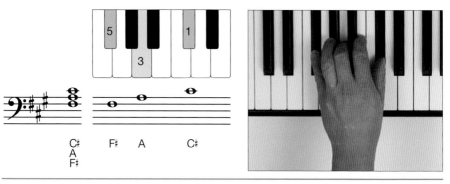

C♯
A
F♯

F♯   A   C♯

1st inversion

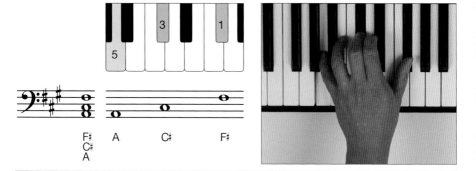

F♯
C♯
A

A   C♯   F♯

2nd inversion

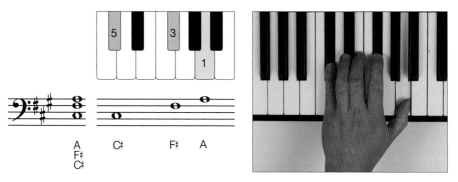

A
F♯
C♯

C♯   F♯   A

F sharp minor
Right hand

Root position

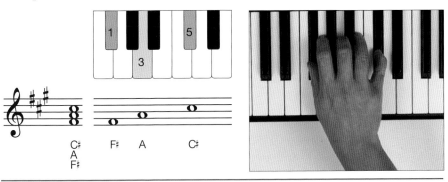

C#
A
F#

F#　A　C#

1st inversion

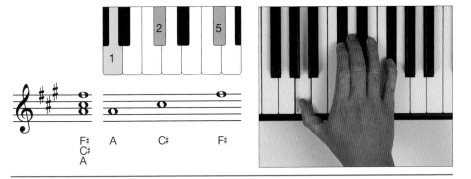

F#
C#
A

A　C#　F#

2nd inversion

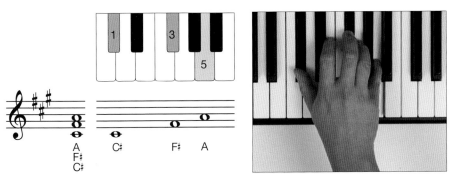

A
F#
C#

C#　F#　A

C sharp minor

Root position

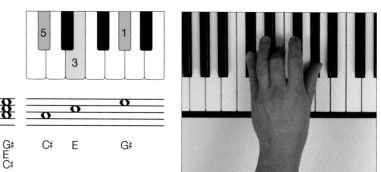

G#
E
C#

C# E G#

1st inversion

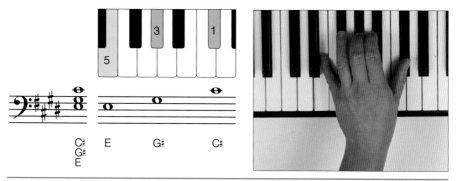

C#
G#
E

E G# C#

2nd inversion

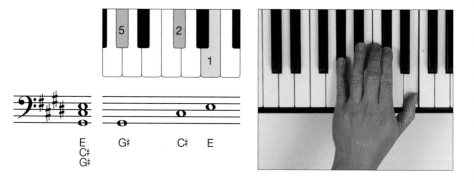

E
C#
G#

G# C# E

C sharp minor   Right hand

Root position

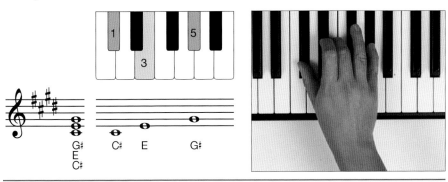

G#
E
C#

C#   E   G#

1st inversion

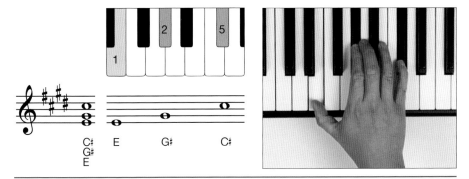

C#
G#
E

E   G#   C#

2nd inversion

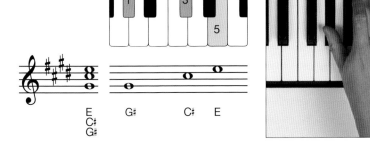

E
C#
G#

G#   C#   E

Left hand

G sharp minor

Root position

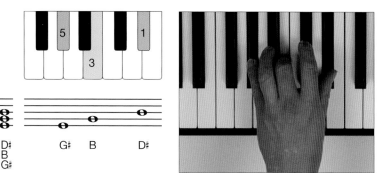

D#
B
G#

G#   B   D#

1st inversion

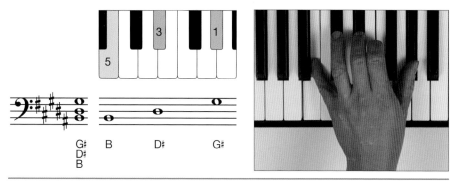

G#
D#
B

G#   B   D#   G#

2nd inversion

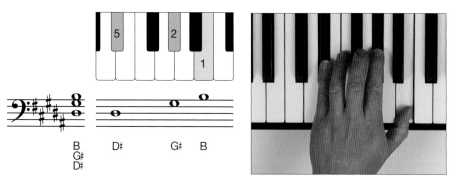

B
G#
D#

D#   G#   B

G sharp minor

Root position

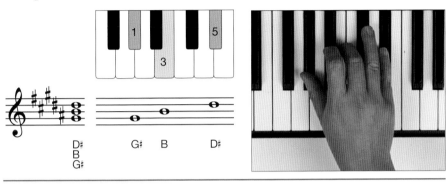

D#
B
G#

G#   B   D#

1st inversion

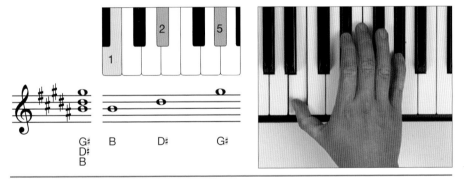

G#
D#
B

B   D#   G#

2nd inversion

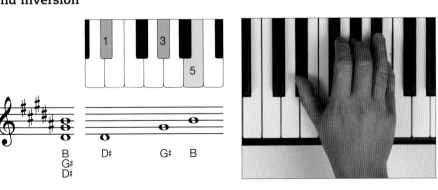

B
G#
D#

D#   G#   B

E flat minor

Root position

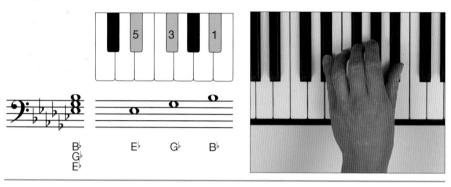

B♭
G♭
E♭

E♭ G♭ B♭

1st inversion

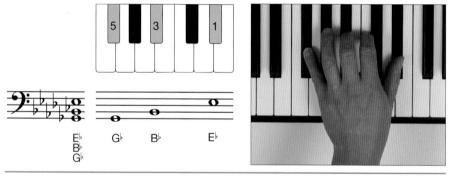

E♭
B♭
G♭

G♭ B♭ E♭

2nd inversion

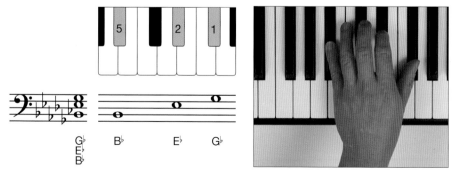

G♭
E♭
B♭

B♭ E♭ G♭

E flat minor Right hand

Root position

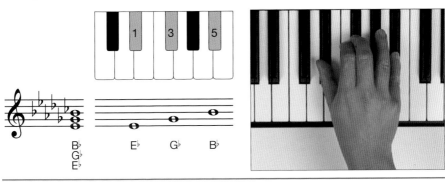

Bᵇ
Gᵇ
Eᵇ

Eᵇ　　Gᵇ　　Bᵇ

1st inversion

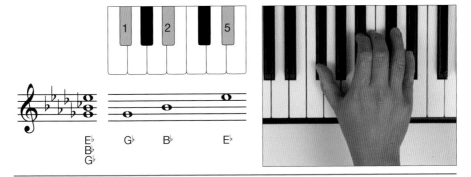

Eᵇ
Bᵇ
Gᵇ

Gᵇ　　Bᵇ　　Eᵇ

2nd inversion

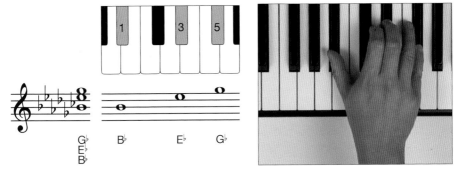

Gᵇ
Eᵇ
Bᵇ

Bᵇ　　Eᵇ　　Gᵇ

B flat minor

Root position

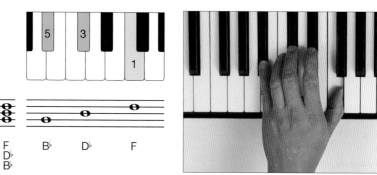

F	B♭	D♭	F
D♭			
B♭			

1st inversion

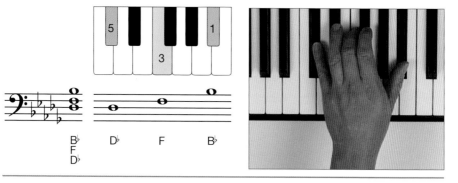

B♭	D♭	F	B♭
F			
D♭			

2nd inversion

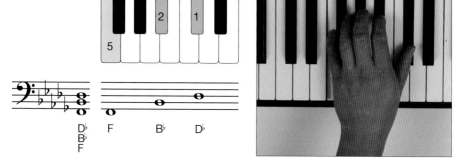

D♭	F	B♭	D♭
B♭			
F			

B flat minor

Root position

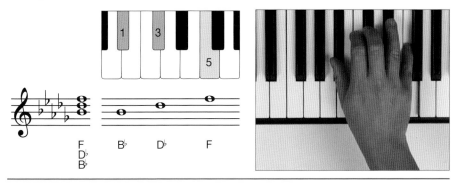

F
D♭
B♭

B♭   D♭   F

1st inversion

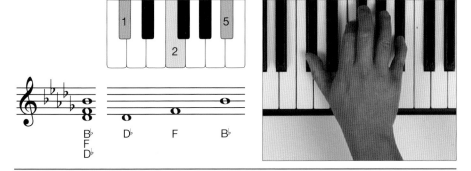

B♭
F
D♭

D♭   F   B♭

2nd inversion

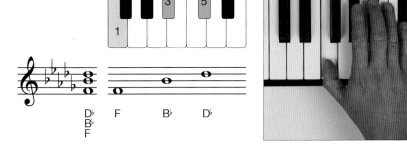

D♭
B♭
F

F   B♭   D♭

F minor

Root position

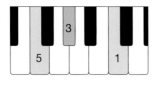

C
A♭
F

F   A♭   C

1st inversion

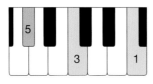

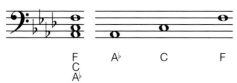

F
C
A♭

A♭   C   F

2nd inversion

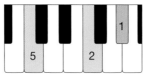

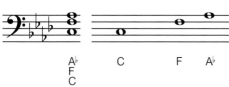

A♭
F
C

C   F   A♭

F minor

Root position

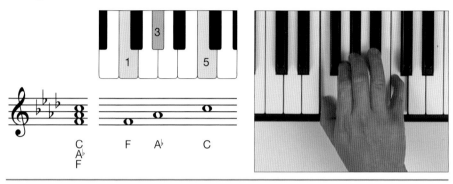

C
A♭
F

F A♭ C

1st inversion

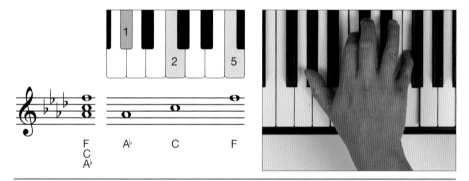

F
C
A♭

A♭ C F

2nd inversion

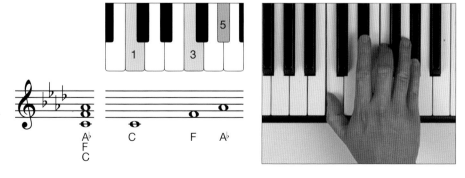

A♭
A
F
C

C F A♭

C minor

Root position

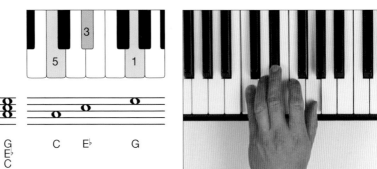

G
E♭
C

C   E♭   G

1st inversion

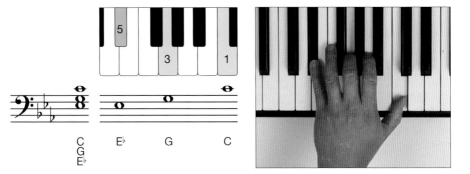

C
G
E♭

E♭   G   C

2nd inversion

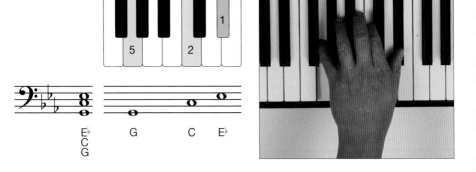

E♭
C
G

G   C   E♭

C minor

Root position

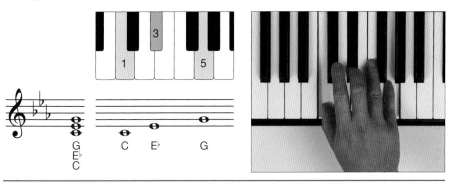

G
E♭
C

C   E♭   G

1st inversion

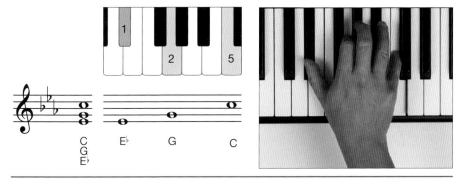

C
G
E♭

E♭   G   C

2nd inversion

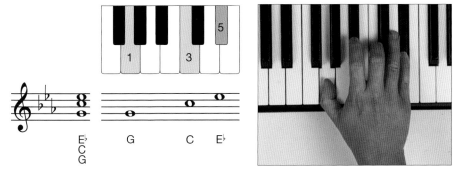

E♭
C
G

G   C   E♭

G minor

Root position

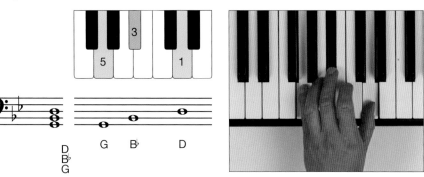

D
B♭
G

G   B♭   D

1st inversion

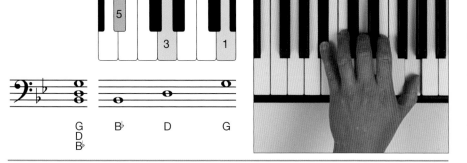

G
D
B♭

B♭   D   G

2nd inversion

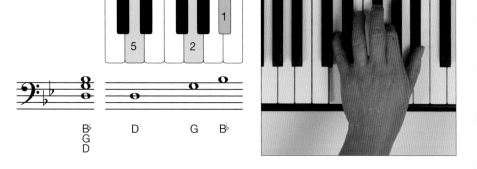

B♭
G
D

D   G   B♭

G minor

Root position

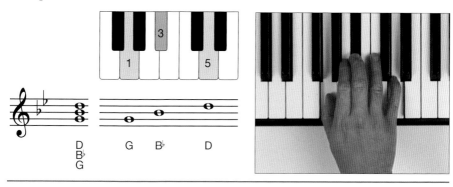

D
B♭
G

G   B♭   D

1st inversion

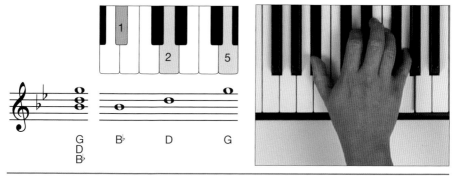

G
D
B♭

B♭   D   G

2nd inversion

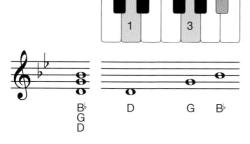
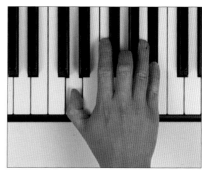

B♭
G
D

D   G   B♭

D minor

Root position

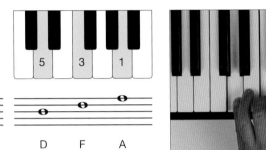

A F D   D   F   A

1st inversion

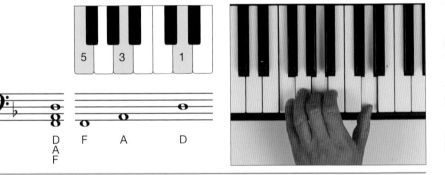

D A F   F   A   D

2nd inversion

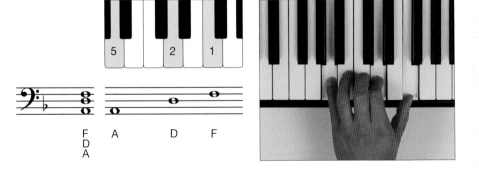

F D A   A   D   F

D minor

Root position

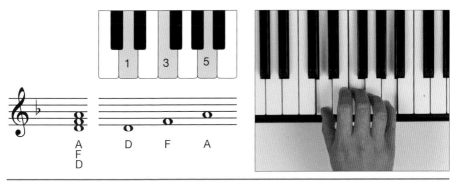

A
F
D

D   F   A

1st inversion

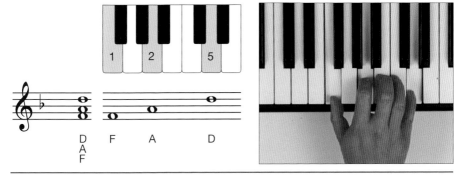

D
A
F

F   A   D

2nd inversion

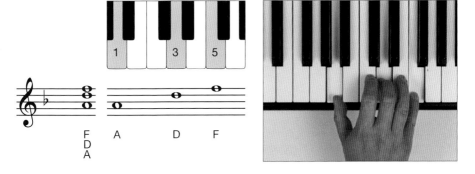

F
D
A

A   D   F

Scale Library

This section provides the notation, and diagrams, for all major and minor scales. It is designed to be a reference tool and also a way of encouraging you to include scales in your regular practice. Regular practice will increase your knowledge of different keys, and strengthen your fingers.

Remember—boxers skip, musicians play scales.

Introduction to scales

Before we dive into the scale library let's have a closer look at the actual technique involved in playing scales.

Right hand

Finger number: 1 2 3 1 2 3 4 1 2 3 1 2 3 4 5

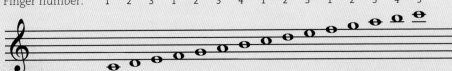

Note names: C D E F G A B C D E F G A B C

The right hand thumb starts on middle C. Keep your fingers curved and wrist level.

Third finger plays A. Lift your finger from the knuckle and play with your fingertips.

As you play B with the fourth finger your thumb comes under to start the second octave.

Left hand

Finger number: 5 4 3 2 1 3 2 1 4 3 2 1 3 2 1

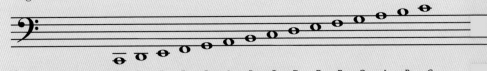

Note names: C D E F G A B C D E F G A B C

As you play this C your fourth finger begins to cross over.

Hold the C until your fourth finger crosses over to play the D.

As you play the D with your fourth finger hand returns to normal.

Practicing scales is a great way of improving your technique, especially in terms of developing finger strength and speed. Because scales are less demanding creatively, you can focus more on technical matters such as posture and hand position. Always aim for an even tone and a steady pulse and gradually speed them up as you gain confidence.

4 3 2 1 3 2 1 4 3 2 1 3 2 1

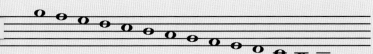

B A G F E D C B A G F E D C

As you play the F with your thumb start to cross your third finger over the top.

Keep holding the F with your thumb until you actually play the E with the third finger.

As you play the D with your second finger your thumb comes back under.

2 3 1 2 3 4 1 2 3 1 2 3 4 5

B A G F E D C B A G F E D C

Your thumb comes under your fingers as you play the A with the third finger.

Your fingers cross over as you play the G with your thumb.

Your hand returns to a normal position as you play the F with your second finger.

C major

Right hand

Left hand

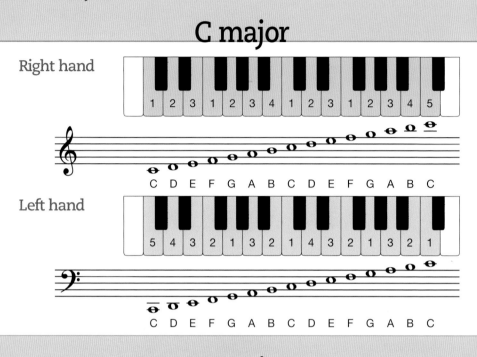

G major

Right hand

Left hand

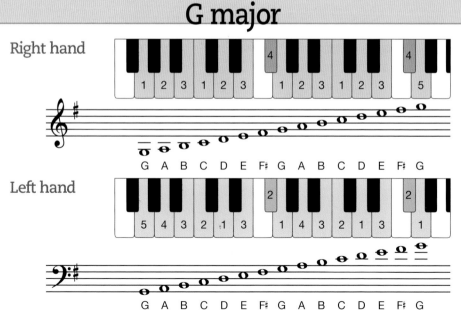

D major

Right hand

Left hand

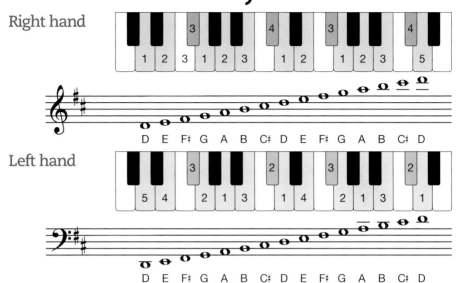

A major

Right hand

Left hand

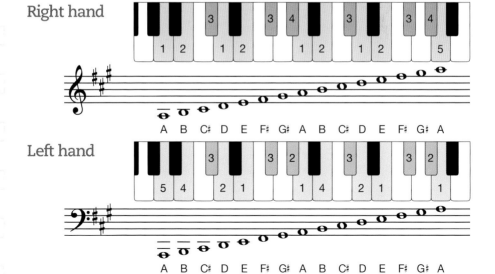

E major

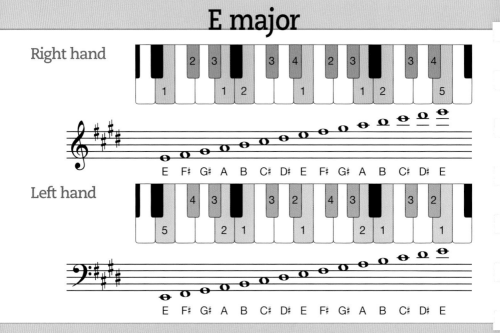

Right hand

E F♯ G♯ A B C♯ D♯ E F♯ G♯ A B C♯ D♯ E

Left hand

E F♯ G♯ A B C♯ D♯ E F♯ G♯ A B C♯ D♯ E

B major

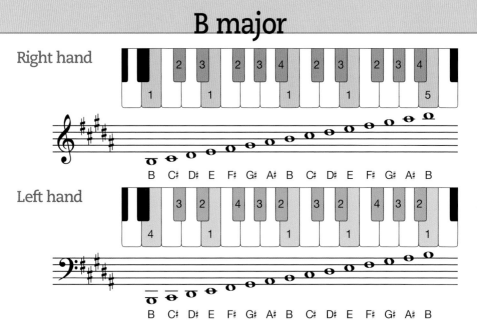

Right hand

B C♯ D♯ E F♯ G♯ A♯ B C♯ D♯ E F♯ G♯ A♯ B

Left hand

B C♯ D♯ E F♯ G♯ A♯ B C♯ D♯ E F♯ G♯ A♯ B

G flat major (also known as F sharp major)

Right hand

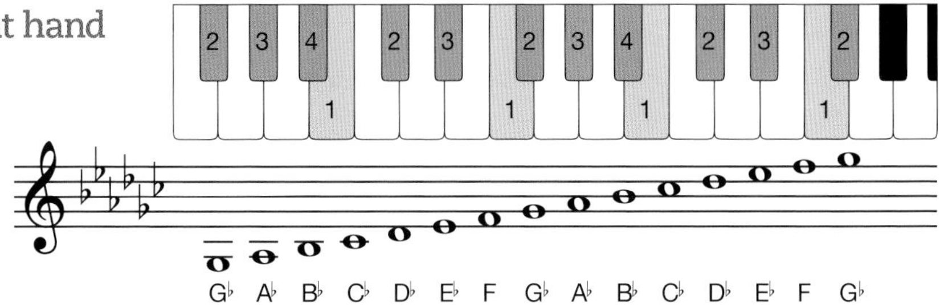

2 3 4 2 3 2 3 4 2 3 2
1 1 1 1
G♭ A♭ B♭ C♭ D♭ E♭ F G♭ A♭ B♭ C♭ D♭ E♭ F G♭

Left hand

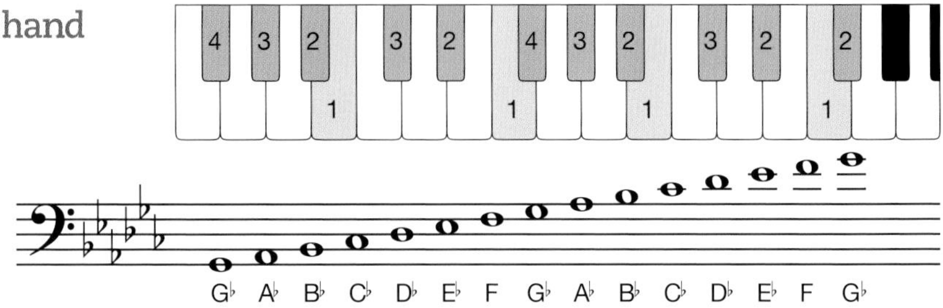

4 3 2 3 2 4 3 2 3 2 2
1 1 1 1
G♭ A♭ B♭ C♭ D♭ E♭ F G♭ A♭ B♭ C♭ D♭ E♭ F G♭

D flat major

Right hand

2 3 2 3 4 2 3 2 3 4 2
1 1 1 1
D♭ E♭ F G♭ A♭ B♭ C D♭ E♭ F G♭ A♭ B♭ C D♭

Left hand

3 2 4 3 2 3 2 4 3 2 2
1 1 1 1
D♭ E♭ F G♭ A♭ B♭ C D♭ E♭ F G♭ A♭ B♭ C D♭

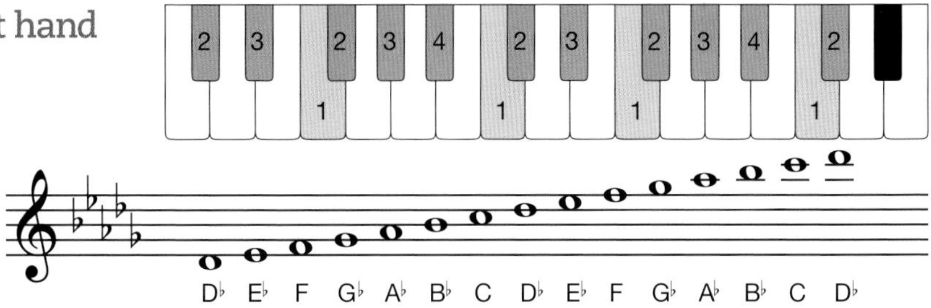

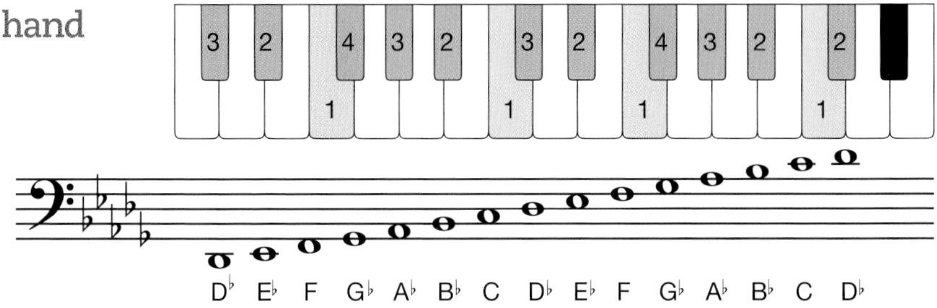

A flat Major

Right hand

Left hand

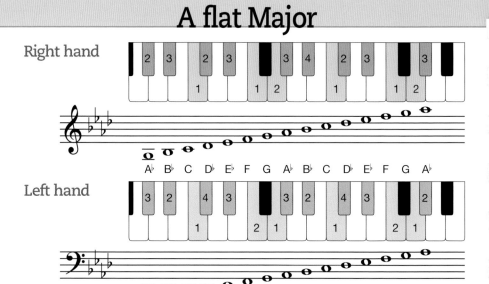

E flat major

Right hand

Left hand

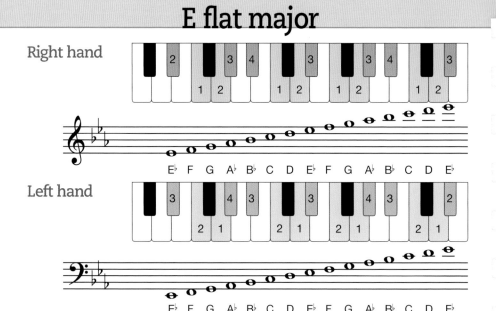

B flat major

Right hand

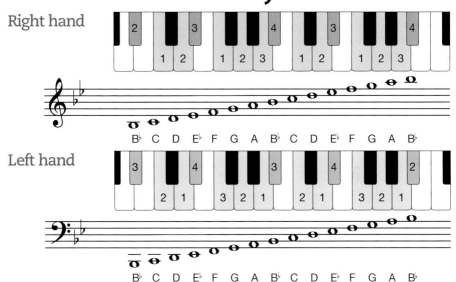

Left hand

F major

Right hand

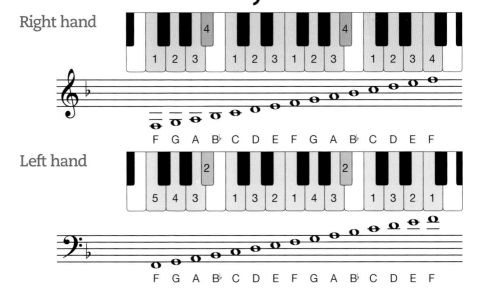

Left hand

A minor

Right hand

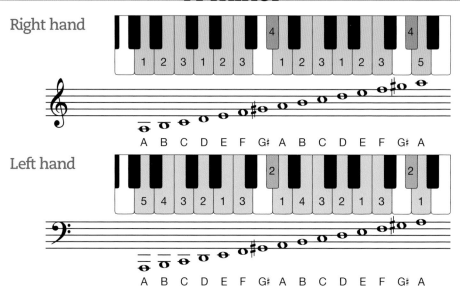

A B C D E F G♯ A B C D E F G♯ A

Left hand

A B C D E F G♯ A B C D E F G♯ A

E minor

Right hand

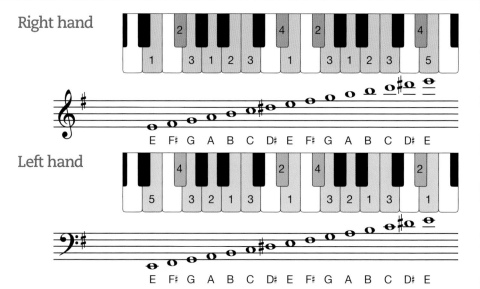

E F♯ G A B C D♯ E F♯ G A B C D♯ E

Left hand

E F♯ G A B C D♯ E F♯ G A B C D♯ E

B minor

Right hand

Left hand

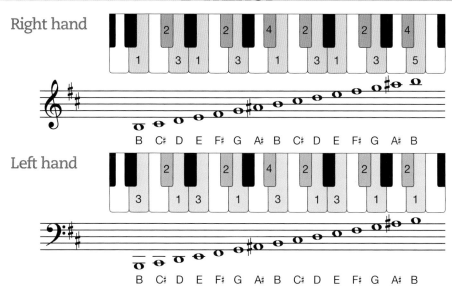

F sharp minor

Right hand

Left hand

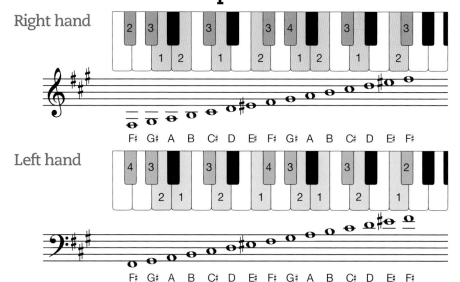

C sharp minor

Right hand

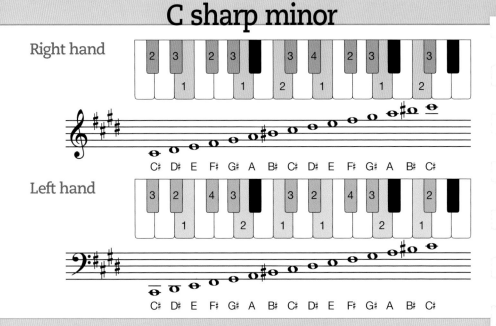

Left hand

G sharp minor

Right hand

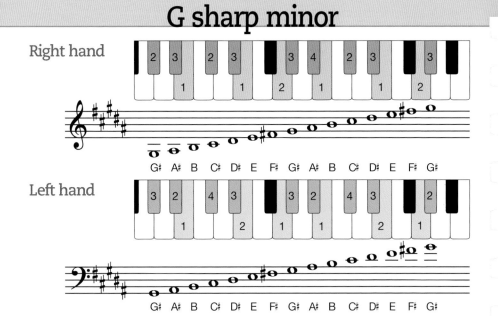

Left hand

E flat minor

Right hand

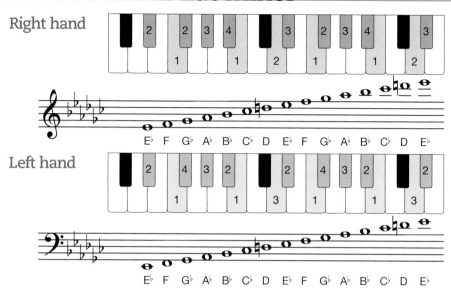

E♭ F G♭ A♭ B♭ C♭ D E♭ F G♭ A♭ B♭ C♭ D E♭

Left hand

E♭ F G♭ A♭ B♭ C♭ D E♭ F G♭ A♭ B♭ C♭ D E♭

B flat minor

Right hand

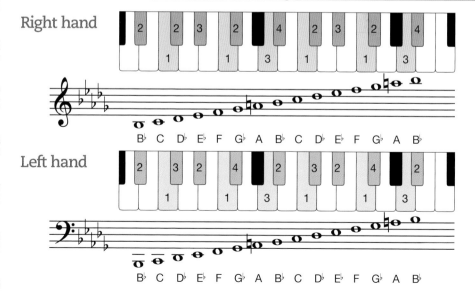

B♭ C D♭ E♭ F G♭ A B♭ C D♭ E♭ F G♭ A B♭

Left hand

B♭ C D♭ E♭ F G♭ A B♭ C D♭ E♭ F G♭ A B♭

F minor

Right hand

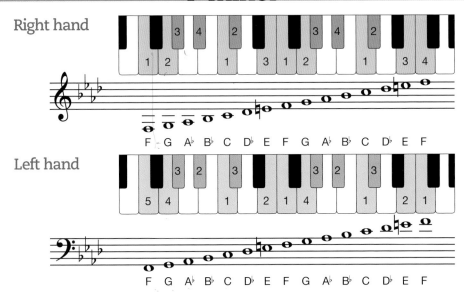

Left hand

C minor

Right hand

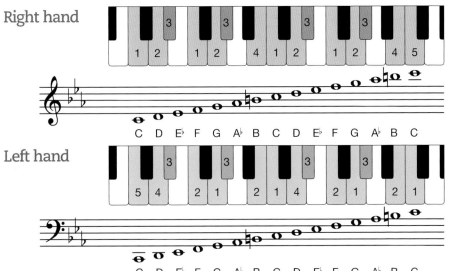

Left hand

G minor

Right hand

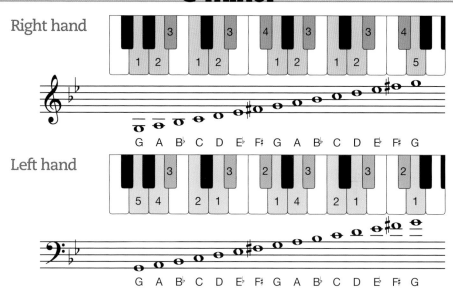

G A B♭ C D E♭ F♯ G A B♭ C D E♭ F♯ G

Left hand

G A B♭ C D E♭ F♯ G A B♭ C D E♭ F♯ G

D minor

Right hand

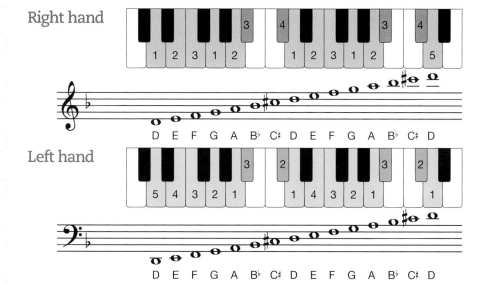

D E F G A B♭ C♯ D E F G A B♭ C♯ D

Left hand

D E F G A B♭ C♯ D E F G A B♭ C♯ D

A Brief History of Keyboards

This section explores the evolution of the keyboard in twentieth-century music, and charts the artists who embraced the new technology, from the 1930s until the 1990s.

Herbie Hancock with Yamaha, left

Hammond Organ

The facts

The story of the Hammond Organ began in 1934 when Laurens Hammond invented an electrical organ to recreate the sound of a church pipe-organ. Over the next twenty years the instrument was tweaked and refined, and in 1955 the most famous version, the B3, was released.

Jimmy Smith, poised to play the Hammond Organ—London, during the early 1960s.

The sound of the Hammond Organ is generated by a tone-wheel that rotates over an electromagnetic coil and is then amplified. Part of the classic Hammond Organ sound is created by a Leslie speaker, which rotates inside the cabinet to produce a rich chorus or tremolo effect.

A system of drawbars emulates the stops on a pipe-organ and enables the organist to blend the harmonics of each note to create a rich variety of timbres. The last tone-wheel organs were produced in the mid 1970s, and subsequent designs use electronic oscillators and digital technology to replicate their sound. Many people still prefer the old tone-wheel sound and vintage models are still in use today.

The musicians

The Hammond Organ was originally sold to churches as a low-cost and portable alternative to a pipe-organ, but it was also used widely in theaters. In the 1950s, jazz musicians such as **Jimmy McGriff** and **Jimmy Smith** used the Hammond Organ, often in a trio setting, as the instrument enabled them to play bass lines, chords, and melodies all at once. This appealed to bar and club owners who could pay one musician for doing the job of two or three.

In the late 1960s and early 1970s, rock bands **Deep Purple** and **Led Zeppelin** used the sound of the Hammond Organ, as did **Genesis**, **Pink Floyd**, and **Emerson, Lake, and Palmer**.

The Hammond Organ is a great all-rounder and can fit into any genre—gospel, blues, reggae, jazz, and soul to name but a few. Just about any band with a keyboard player will have used a Hammond Organ at one time or another.

Wurlitzer Electric Piano

The facts

The action of the Wurlitzer piano is a miniature version of a grand piano, and the sound source is a single steel reed for each key, which is amplified using an electromagnetic pick-up system. The Wurlitzer featured a built-in tremolo control with a knob to control the intensity of the effect, which became an instantly recognizable sound.

Noel Gallagher and Paul Weller performing Oasis' "Talk Tonight" on Channel 4's "The White Room," April 14, 1995.

The Wurlitzer has a sweet, vibraphone-like tone when played gently, but when played harder, it becomes harsher and develops an over-driven type of distortion.

Most preset "electric piano" voices on contemporary keyboards are based on either a Wurlitzer or a Fender Rhodes electric piano.

The Wurlitzer Company originally manufactured pipe-organs for churches and theaters, and later produced jukeboxes and electric pianos. The first Wurlitzer electric pianos were produced in 1955 and production continued until 1982.

The musicians

A 1956 recording by the jazz keyboard pioneer Sun Ra is claimed to be the earliest featuring a Wurlitzer. However "What'd I Say," released by **Ray Charles** in 1959, is one of the most famous recorded examples of the instrument. In the 1960s and 1970s the Wurlitzer was used by anyone who wanted an electric piano (there weren't that many options at that time).

Some better-known excursions are:

"Chinese Checkers"
Booker T. and the M.G.s
"See the Sky About to Rain" **Neil Young**
"Lazy Sunday" **The Small Faces**
"Woodstock" **Joni Mitchell**
"Top of the World" **The Carpenters**
"The Logical Song" **Supertramp**
"Godwhacker" **Steely Dan**
"You're My Best Friend" **Queen**
"I Heard it Through the Grapevine"
Marvin Gaye
"Money" **Pink Floyd**

Vox Continental

The facts

The Vox Continental is an electronic organ that was released in 1962. It was designed to be a replacement for the heavier and less portable tone-wheel organs, of which the Hammond B3 is the most well known.

Although it never really succeeded in replicating the sound of the Hammond Organ, the Vox Continental created its own sonic landscape. It was enormously popular throughout the 1960s and 1970s, as it was designed primarily for stage work, and was so much more portable than its tone-wheel rivals. The Vox Continental had a look all of its own with reversed white and black keys, a bright red casing, and a unique Z-frame stand.

There were single and dual manual versions, and later models called the Vox Jaguar and the Vox Corinthian, but they all shared the same look and sound.

The musicians

The most famous recording of a Vox Continental is arguably "The House of the Rising Sun" by **The Animals**, and another famous example is "I'm a Believer" by **The Monkees**. **Ray Manzarek** of **The Doors** used one extensively. "Watching the Detectives" and "Go to Chelsea" by **Elvis Costello And The Attractions** both feature the Vox Continental and 1980s chart regulars **Madness** frequently used one.

Left to right: Hilton Valentine, Alan Price, Eric Burdon, John Steel, and Chas Chandler from The Animals, performing on "Ready Steady Go!" at Television House, Kingsway in 1964.

Fender Rhodes

The facts

The Rhodes electric piano was invented during the Second World War when Harold Rhodes was asked to provide music therapy for wounded soldiers. Originally created using surplus Air Force parts, it emerged in its now-familiar form in 1965.

The musicians

One of the earliest recordings of a Rhodes piano is the 1968 **Miles Davis** album *Miles in the Sky* which features **Herbie Hancock** playing the instrument. **Herbie Hancock** became a huge fan of the Rhodes piano and inspired many other jazz and fusion musicians such as **Chick Corea** and **Joe Zawinul** to use it.

Ray Charles can be seen playing a Rhodes piano on "Shake a Tail Feather" in the 1980 film *The Blues Brothers* and has used it on many other recordings.

Other artists who have used the Rhodes sound include:

Stevie Wonder, The Doors, Pink Floyd, Billy Joel, Radiohead, R.E.M., Tupac, and **Erykah Badu.**

The characteristic sound is produced by a hammer hitting a stiff wire (called a "tine") which causes a tuned metal block to resonate. The vibrations are then picked up by an electromagnetic coil similar to a guitar pick-up, and amplified. The resulting sound blends a clear, bell-like quality and a long, atmospheric sustain.

Ray Charles playing a Rhodes electric—Newport Jazz Festival, 1973.

Mellotron

The facts

The Mellotron is a keyboard instrument that uses prerecorded tapes to produce its sound. It is basically an early type of sampler where the samples are not digital, but recorded onto tape. Each note on the keyboard triggers a separate tape section with a prerecorded sound on it. Different banks of tapes have different instruments recorded onto them, such as strings or flute.

David Cross (far left) playing the Mellotron with fellow musicians (left to right): John Wetton, Bill Bruford, and Robert Fripp (with Mellotron), performing on a French TV show in Paris, March 22, 1974.

The first Mellotrons were produced in England in the mid 1960s based on an earlier type of tape-playing keyboard instrument developed in the United States. The characteristics and imperfections of tape-recorded sound give the Mellotron its unique quality, but are also responsible for some of its failings— unreliable tuning being its main drawback.

The musicians

The Mellotron was used extensively by rock bands in the 1960s and 1970s. **The Beatles** used one on "Strawberry Fields Forever," recorded in 1966, and **The Moody Blues'** classic "Nights in White Satin" features the haunting tones of a Mellotron. Other artists of that era to use a Mellotron include **The Kinks, Marvin Gaye, The Bee Gees, The Rolling Stones,** and **David Bowie**.

In the late 1970s, more reliable and cheaper synthesizers and dedicated string machines gradually took over from the Mellotron. It has enjoyed renewed popularity of late, with bands like **Smashing Pumpkins, Oasis,** and **Radiohead** using a Mellotron.

Hohner Clavinet

The facts

The Clavinet is based on the Clavichord, and is mechanically very similar, with the advantage that the sound can be amplified and manipulated. Unlike a piano, the hammer does not strike the strings, but "frets" them in the same way as a "hammer-on" in guitar-playing (picking the string only once, but producing two or more notes.)

The result is a different type of attack and a completely different timbre to the note. The vibrations of the string are amplified using electromagnetic coils similarly to the Fender Rhodes and Wurlitzer electric pianos. The Clavinet was originally designed for European classical and folk music and was built for domestic use with a wooden case and legs. Later models were adapted to be more suitable for playing amplified rock music and were far more robust.

Stevie Wonder rocking the charts with his Clavinet solo on "Top Of The Pops," c.1972.

The musicians

Stevie Wonder is undoubtedly the man responsible for popularizing the Hohner Clavinet, on his recordings "Superstition" and "Higher Ground" in particular. He used the percussive quality of the instrument to great rhythmic effect, and it has ever-after been associated with funky rhythmic patterns. The "clav" and "funky clav" family of presets are all based on the Hohner Clavinet as played by Stevie Wonder. Other famous recordings featuring a Clavinet are: "Machine Gun," by **The Commodores**, "Nut Rocker" by **Emerson, Lake, and Palmer**, and *Head Hunters*, the 1973 album by **Herbie Hancock**.

Minimoog

The facts

The Minimoog is a monophonic analog synthesizer that was released in 1970 and was one of the first easily available and portable instruments of its kind. It excels at producing rich lead sounds and fat, powerful bass sounds, which is why it is still very much in demand.

The Minimoog has three oscillators and a noise-generator, which are controlled by a powerful filter to create the unique sound. To the left of the keyboard are a pitch-bend wheel and a modulation wheel, which can create very expressive performance.

Chick Corea and his Minimoog, performing in London, c.1975.

The musicians

The Minimoog has always been a favorite with jazz fusion keyboard players such as **Herbie Hancock, Joe Zawinul**, and **Chick Corea**. In 1974 the band **Kraftwerk** used it extensively on their revolutionary and massively influential album *Autobahn*.

In the 1980s, **Ultravox** and **Depeche Mode** were using the Minimoog to create the electronic pop of that era. **The Orb** and **The Chemical Brothers** are examples of contemporary artists for whom the Minimoog is indispensable.

ARP Odyssey

The facts

The ARP Odyssey was launched in 1972, and was the first challenge to the Minimoog's supremacy in the affordable, portable synthesizer market. ARP had produced two previous synthesizers in 1970—the ARP 2500 and the ARP 2600—both of which were vast, massively complicated instruments.

The ARP 2800, named the "Odyssey," was a simplified version of the earlier 2600, and was instantly recognizable, with a white control panel and multicolored sliders. In many areas the Odyssey compared unfavorably with the Minimoog; it had no pitch-bend or modulation wheels, but the quality of sound was right up there with the Minimoog. Generally, the Odyssey is considered to have a harsher, more aggressive sound than the Minimoog, which is famed for its warmth.

In 1977, ARP released an updated version of the Odyssey with various "improvements" and a new color scheme. There were four later models but they were all known as the Mark 2.

The musicians

Jazz fusion pioneers **Herbie Hancock** and **Joe Zawinul** were early experimenters with the Odyssey. Just about any keyboard player in the 1970s and early 1980s would have used one at some time or another. These are some of the most famous examples:

"Oxygene"
Jean-Michel Jarre

"Rocket Man"
Elton John

"Blinded By The Light"
Manfred Mann's Earth Band

"Undertow" and "Leave"
from *New Adventures in Hi-Fi*
R.E.M.

Pioneer of the ARP Odyssey, Jon Lord of Deep Purple, on a U.S. tour, 1974.

Prophet 5

The facts

In 1978, a company called Sequential Circuits produced the groundbreaking Prophet 5. This analog synthesizer was polyphonic and could play five notes simultaneously, which at the time was a massive improvement on other affordable synths.

The other outstanding feature of the Prophet 5 was that it could store patches; that is, it would scan all the parameter settings and store them in a memory, which could be recalled when needed. This facility is taken for granted today, but in previous synthesizers all parameters had to be manually set up, which meant you really needed to know what was what, especially in a gigging situation.

The musicians

The Prophet 5 has been used extensively by many famous artists, among others:

Roxy Music on "Flesh and Blood" and "Avalon." **Kraftwerk, Duran Duran, Peter Gabriel, Gary Numan** (who had four on stage at one time,) **Jean-Michel Jarre, The Eurythmics, Genesis, Soft Cell, Hall and Oates**, and **David Bowie**.

The Prophet 5 (left) makes a prominent appearance at a Talking Heads gig in Central Park, NYC, 1980.

Fairlight CMI

The facts

The Fairlight CMI (Computer Musical Instrument) was the first polyphonic keyboard that used digital sampling technology. It was created in Australia by the Fairlight Company and released in 1980 after years of research. As well as its sampling capabilities, the CMI had a graphic sequencer, a software-based synthesizer, and introduced the concept of multi-timbrality, all of which became standard features of the workstation.

The musicians

Although the CMI's price put it out of reach of just about everybody, established artists and producers did use them. **Peter Gabriel** was one of the first to get one in the UK and one of the first recordings was **Kate Bush's** 1980 album *Never For Ever*. Producer **Trevor Horn** used a CMI on the Frankie Goes To Hollywood hit "Relax," and **Jan Hammer's** video of the theme from *Miami Vice* features one.

The Fairlight CMI was hand-built to a very high specification and wasn't cheap, coming in at around $40,000. The Series II was released in 1982 and had increased processor power, as well as an increased price tag of about $55,000.

At the time, the Fairlight CMI, with its white casing and graphic screen control really seemed to represent the future of music technology.

Jan Hammer showcasing the Fairlight CMI in 1987.

E-MU Emulator

The facts

The E-MU (Electronic Music) Company, based in California, had been producing modular synthesizer systems throughout the 1970s, and were one of the first companies to latch onto the new sampling technology that the Fairlight CMI had brought into the public consciousness.

The Emulator I was a "bargain-basement" sampler, costing a mere $10,000 on its release in 1981, and the Emulator II, released in 1984, was even cheaper at $7,995. The Emulator II had several innovations including a multitrack MIDI (see Glossary, page 250) sequencer, and analog filters. A company called Digidesign developed a software product to support the Emulator II that ran on newly released Macintosh computers and paved the way for computer and keyboard-integrated systems.

The musicians

Stevie Wonder received the very first production Emulator I, with serial number 001.

In the Live Aid concert of 1985, **Ultravox** and **Dire Straits** both used an Emulator II on stage, and in the same year **Paul Hardcastle's** No. 1 hit "19" used an Emulator II to create the unsettling repetition of the title.

Neil Tennant (left) and Chris Lowe (right) performing on Channel 4's "The Tube" in 1986.

Roland Jupiter 8

The facts

The Jupiter 8 was produced between 1981 and 1985, and was probably the last polyphonic analog synthesizer to make an impact before the arrival of sampling and other digital audio technologies. The Jupiter 8 has an incredible array of colored buttons, sliders, switches, and knobs and is a marvelous object to behold. It is the most solid and reliable of all the "polysynths" and is still in frequent use today.

The Jupiter 8 incorporated Roland's own-brand DCB synchronizing system, that enabled it to be linked up with other Roland products, such as the TR808 and TR909 drum machines. The debate had long raged as to whether the Japanese synth manufacturers such as Korg, Roland, and Casio ever produced anything with the sonic muscle of the U.S.-produced Minimoog and Prophet 5, and the arrival of the Jupiter 8 aggravated the debate.

The musicians

The Jupiter 8 was used widely throughout the 1980s and 1990s. Here are some of its most famous appearances:

"Hungry Like the Wolf"
Duran Duran
"Axel F" (theme from *Beverley Hills Cop*)
Harold Faltermeyer
"Thriller" **Michael Jackson**
"Radio Gaga"(The bass line was created using the Jupiter 8 arpeggiator) and "I Want to Break Free" (The keyboard solo was performed on a Jupiter 8)
Queen

Others notable users include **Tears for Fears, Depeche Mode, Jean-Michel Jarre, Howard Jones, Foreigner,** and **Rush.**

Greg Hawkes of U.S. punk band The Cars tinkering with the Jupiter 8, c.1983.

Yamaha CP-70

The facts

Various attempts have been made to build a portable piano that can be amplified, the most successful being the Fender Rhodes and the Wurlitzer, although neither of these actually sounds like a real piano. In the mid 1970s Yamaha released the CP-70 "Electric Grand Piano," which featured a genuine grand piano action and real strings on an iron frame.

The CP-70 used special strings so that there didn't have to be as many as on a real grand piano, which reduced the weight. To make it more portable, the CP-70 broke down into two boxes, one with the frame and strings; the other with the keyboard and legs. However, it is extremely heavy and the portability claim is debatable. The CP-70 is the closest that anyone has come to making an electric piano that sounds like a real piano, and definitely has a sound and personality of its own.

The musicians

Peter Gabriel, **Abba**, **U2**, and **Simple Minds** have all used a Yamaha CP-70. **John Paul Jones** of **Led Zeppelin** had one made with a white case to look like a real grand piano.

More recently, **Keane** have made the CP-70 an integral part of their sound and one of the instruments even features on the band's website.

Tim Rice-Oxley of Keane rocking out on the Electric Grand in 2007 at Brixton Academy, London.

DX7

The facts

The Yamaha DX7 was released in 1983 and was the first commercially successful digital synthesizer. The sounds are created using a system called FM synthesis, and are characterized by clear metallic and bell-like sounds, although the DX7 can produce all kinds of weird effects as well as thick analog-type sounds.

Herbie Hancock performing in New York, 1988.

The DX7 was precise and reliable, and for keyboard players who were used to grappling with the unreliability and idiosyncratic performance of analog synths, it was just what they had been waiting for. However, the DX7 is extremely difficult to program as the sounds are generated by algorithms that respond unpredictably to "tweaking," and the whole procedure is negotiated via a small screen and 32 membrane-covered buttons. Several later versions were produced with comprehensive MIDI (see Glossary, page 250) spec and various other excellent improvements.

The DX7 sounds outdated to modern ears, but if used in the right context with the right effects, it can still pack a punch. Because of their solid construction and reliable circuitry there are many still around and they can be a secondhand bargain.

The musicians

At this stage in the development of keyboards, it becomes difficult to associate the DX7 with any particular artists because any band with a keyboard player would have used a DX7, and just about any commercial studio would have owned one. Some of the most famous artists who have used a DX7 are: **Jan Hammer** (on *Miami Vice*), **The Cure, The Beastie Boys, Depeche Mode, Brian Eno, Kool and the Gang, Madonna, Talking Heads, U2,** the massively successful production team **Stock, Aitken and Waterman, Underworld, Enya, Herbie Hancock, Sting,** and **Queen.**

Synthesizers

Synthesizers occupy a rather specialized niche in the keyboard market these days. Many hark back to the glory days of analog synths, with names derivative of vintage classics, and retro styling to evoke the look of synths of the 1970s and 1980s.

Sampling technology means that a keyboard can produce a vast palette of sounds without actually generating them; they already exist in sampled form and are triggered by the keyboard. There are modern synthesizers that use genuine sound-generating technology, combined with sampling technology, and are capable of producing an incredible range and depth of sounds.

Because of the technology involved, these keyboards can seem expensive for the features they offer, but they are something of a niche market.

Access, Alesis, Clavia, Korg, Novation, and Roland all produce ranges of keyboard synthesizers.

Roland SH-201
Synthesizer

Invisible infrared D-beam
controler for dramatic modulation

Delay and reverb effects for
adding depth and dimension

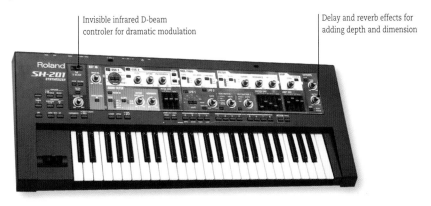

USB port for audio/MIDI
connection to computer

Workstations

Workstations are keyboards that incorporate synthesizer functions, sampling capability, multitrack sequencers, computer interfaces, arpeggiators… and lots of other things involving large numbers and initials.

A workstation is a powerful tool for creating sounds, sequencing tracks, and a whole lot besides, and this is reflected in the price. It is worth considering how many of the features you are actually going to use if you are thinking of investing in one.

The main players in this market are Korg and Roland who manufacture models of varying power and price.

Five-octave touch-sensitive keyboard

The LCD screen enables you to navigate through the labyrinth of menus, options, and sub-menus.

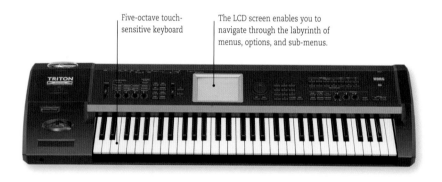

The back panel has a multitude of connections, including audio, midi, and USB interfaces.

The range of features are accessed via data buttons and sliders.

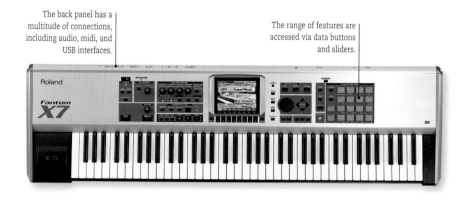

Accessories

There are a few essential items that you will need in order to get started on your keyboard. Here is a quick overview of some useful kit.

Case
The strongest type of case is a flight case, which should protect your keyboard from most knocks, but can be extremely heavy. Another option is a soft "gig-bag," which is lightweight and padded for protection. It's a trade-off between damage to your keyboard and damage to your back!

Amplifier
Unless you have a keyboard with built-in speakers, you will need an amplifier, or "amp." Keyboard amps need to have better bass response than guitar amps because they can play lower notes. The price of an amp depends on its power, size of speaker, and number of other features. Some keyboard amps have multiple inputs, so that you can plug in more than one keyboard, and some of these have separate tone-control settings for each input. Other features to look out for are effects, such as reverb and chorus which can enhance the sound of your keyboard.

Reliable manufacturers of keyboard amps include Hartke, Peavey, Laney, Behringer, Roland, and Yamaha.

Keyboard stand
A keyboard stand means that you can adjust the height of your keyboard to suit the playing situation. Generally the stronger and more solid they are, the less portable they become, so find one to suit your needs. A wobbly stand can be extremely annoying so test it before buying one. Alternately use an old ironing board or decorating table.

Lead
You need a lead to plug your keyboard into the amplifier, and it's worth buying a good-quality one for an improved signal path and greater reliability and longevity.

Glossary

Accidental

Sign that modifies the pitch of the note when placed before it. A sharp (♯), for example, raises a note one semitone; a flat (♭) lowers a note one semitone.

Bass clef

Indicated by the bottom portion of the grand stave, and marked 𝄢, the bass clef dictates the movement of the left hand, and indicates that the fourth line from the bottom of the stave represents the pitch of F below middle C.

Chord

Effect produced by sounding two or more notes together.

Chromatic note

Note that does not belong to the key center being used.

Chromatic scale

12-note scale that goes up, or down, in semitones.

Cycle of fifths

Circular arrangement of the twelve musical notes, moving in fifths clockwise, and fourths anticlockwise.

Comping

Abbreviation for "accompanying," describing the chord pattern used to accompany a singer, or instrumentalist.

Diatonic

A piece of music is described as "diatonic" if its constituent notes are derived from a recognized scale, usually the major, or natural minor scale.

Dominant seventh chord

Major chord (triad) with a fourth note added to a minor third above the fifth. This creates a minor seventh interval from the chord's root note. The chord occurs diatonically on the fifth (V or dominant) degree of the major scale, and resolves naturally to the scale's tonic (I) chord. It is described as a dissonant chord because of the diminished fifth interval between the major third and minor seventh.

Dotted note

Symbol used to indicate an increase of time equal to one half of its simple value, for instance, a dotted whole-note is equal to three half-notes.

Eighth-note, or quaver

Note with the time value of one-eighth of a whole-note.

Flat (♭)

Symbol used to lower the note by one semitone.

Half-note, or minim

Note with the time value of half the length of a whole-note.

Inversion

A chord is inverted if a note other than the root is in its bass. A melody is inverted when it is turned upside down so that the upward movements become equivalent downward movements, and so on.

Key signature

Group of sharps or flats placed to the right of the clef on a stave to identify the key.

Major chord

Most consonant (or stable) chord in music. A triad constructed from the first, third, and fifth degrees of the major scale. Often described as a "happy"-sounding chord.

Measure

Segment of time comprised of a given number of beats of a given duration, as specified by the time signature.

MIDI

Musical Instrument Digital Interface is a system that enables electronic instruments to communicate and synchronize with each other.

Minor chord

Slightly less consonant (or stable) than a major chord due to the relationship between the root (lowest) note of the chord and the minor third. Constructed from the first, third, and fifth degrees of the harmonic minor scale. Often described as a "sad"-sounding chord.

Natural (♮)

Neither sharp nor flat, a natural cancels a preceding accidental and restores the note to its original pitch.

Octave

Interval formed by two notes, of which the upper has twice the frequency of the lower. So called because the upper note forms the eighth note of a diatonic scale commencing on the lower note.

Pentatonic scale

Five-note scale, as formed by the piano's "black notes," with intervals of tones and minor thirds. Widespread in Chinese, African, and Celtic music.

Pitch

"Height" or "depth" of a note as defined by the frequency of its vibrations.

Quarter-note, or crotchet

Note with the time value equal to a quarter of a whole-note. The length of one beat is often written as a quarter-note.

Relative minor

Every major key shares its key signature with a minor key, which is called the relative minor. The tonic of the relative minor is always a minor third lower than that of the major key. For example, the relative minor of D major is B minor, and they share the common key signature of two sharps (F sharp and C sharp).

Rest

Symbol indicating a silence of a definite length.

Riff

Ostinato (or repeated) pattern, usually no more than two bars in length.

Scale

Series of stepwise ascending and descending notes that follow a specific intervallic template of whole (tone) and half (semitone) steps. These are generally seven notes long (i.e. the major scale), but can be shorter (i.e. the five-note pentatonic scale) or longer (i.e. the eight-note diminished scale).

Sharp (♯)

Symbol used to raise the note by one semitone.

Sixteenth-note, or semiquaver

Note with a time value of one sixteenth of a whole-note.

Stave, or staff

Horizontal five-line grid on which musical notes are written to indicate their pitch.

Thirty-second-note, or demi-semiquaver

Note with a time value of one thirty-second of a whole-note.

Time signature

Numerals at beginning of the stave to show measure (or number of beats to the bar), and the time value of each beat. The time signature $\frac{4}{4}$ is called "common time," and can be shown as **c**.

Tone/semitone

Basic unit of measuring the distance between two notes. A tone is equivalent to a whole step, and a semitone a half step.

Treble clef

Indicated by the top portion of the stave, and marked 𝄞, the treble clef traces the movement of the right hand, and locates the G above middle C, placed on the second line of the stave, counting up.

Triad

Chord of three tones, consisting of a given tone with its major or minor third and its perfect, augmented, or diminished fifth.

Triplet

Rhythmic group of three evenly spaced notes played in the time of one or two notes, shown by a "3" under, or over, the notes.

Tied note

Notes of the same pitch with a curved line called a tie joining them(‿). Only the first note is played, and the time value of subsequent tied notes is added on.

Transpose

To translate a composition into a key different to the one in which it was written.

Whole-note, or semibreve

Longest time value in common use, equivalent to two half-notes or four quarter-notes.

Index

Fold-out flap

Use this handy fold-out guide as a quick reference to understanding musical notation.

Middle C

Notation in a nutshell

Treble clef: *Tells you to play the notes with your right hand.*

Timing: *(see page 26) Tells you the time signature. Here, the symbol represents "common time," which is the same as 4/4. The upper number shows how many beats per measure and the lower number represents the note-value of the beat.*

Bar line: *Notation is organized into measures. Bar lines are the vertical lines that separate the measures.*

Flat: *(see page 42) A flat sign indicates that the note must go down a semitone. The symbol may appear at the beginning of a piece of music or next to a particular note (known as an accidental). An accidental continues for the rest of the measure unless a natural sign overrides it.*

Natural: *Indicates the note must be played normally, ignoring the key signature or a previous accidental in the measure.*

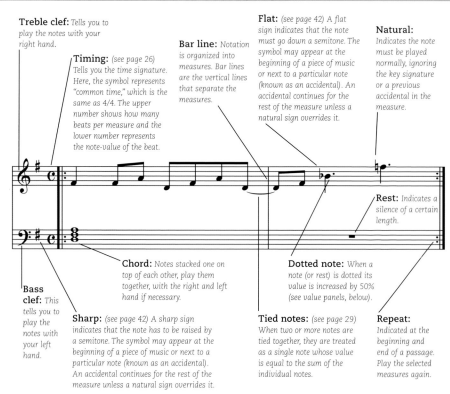

Rest: *Indicates a silence of a certain length.*

Chord: *Notes stacked one on top of each other, play them together, with the right and left hand if necessary.*

Bass clef: *This tells you to play the notes with your left hand.*

Sharp: *(see page 42) A sharp sign indicates that the note has to be raised by a semitone. The symbol may appear at the beginning of a piece of music or next to a particular note (known as an accidental). An accidental continues for the rest of the measure unless a natural sign overrides it.*

Dotted note: *When a note (or rest) is dotted its value is increased by 50% (see value panels, below).*

Tied notes: *(see page 29) When two or more notes are tied together, they are treated as a single note whose value is equal to the sum of the individual notes.*

Repeat: *Indicated at the beginning and end of a passage. Play the selected measures again.*

Note	Value
𝗼·	4 beats
♩	2 beats
♩	1 beat
♪	½ beat
♪	¼ beat
♪	⅛ beat

Rest	Value
▬	4 beats
▬	2 beats
𝄽	1 beat
𝄾	½ beat
𝄿	¼ beat
𝅀	⅛ beat

For more about note and rest values see pages 26–27.

Credits

Quarto would like to acknowledge the following:

IStockphotos 10–11; Ron Howard/Redferns 12; Gilles Petard
Collection/Redferns 71, 85;
David Redfern/Redferns 99, 149, 228, 232, 243; Matt Kent/
Redferns 159; Shutterstock 160–161;
Ebet Roberts/Redferns 226–227, 237, 240, 242; Des Willie/
Redferns 230; Cyrus Andrews/Redferns 231; GAB Archives/
Redferns 233; Ron Howard/Redferns 234; Andrew Putler/
Redferns 235; Fin Costello/Redferns 251; Redferns 238;
Virginia Turbett/Redferns 239; Matt Kent/Redferns 241

Yves Usson
www.casio.co.uk
www.yamaha.com
www.korg.co.uk

All other images are the copyright of Quarto Publishing plc.
While every effort has been made to credit contributors,
Quarto would like to apologize should there be any omissions
or errors—and would be pleased to make the appropriate
correction for future editions of the book.